"This is a powerful story of persistence and personal redemption from one of the leading financial advisors in the history of Northwestern Mutual. Even more, it's a guide for anyone whose aim is to achieve their best and rise to the top. Paul Krasnow's quest to improve the lives of his clients has inspired many inside our company. I'm glad he has chosen to share it with the world."
— **John Schlifske, Chairman and CEO, Northwestern Mutual**

"I first worked for Paul when I was 18 years old. He was the single best salesperson I had ever seen. Of course, I was a young man—but now that I'm older and much more experienced, I still think that. Why? Not only does he know his craft, but he also knows his clients and knows how to connect the two in a meaningful way. He's an amazing connector! When I started Westwood One, I immediately put him on the board. We saw him as much more than our insurance guy. To us, he was a consummate business professional and a trusted advisor."
— **Norman J. Pattiz, Founder of Radio Network Westwood One, Member of the National Radio Hall of Fame**

"I have been fortunate to have Paul as a trusted advisor and friend for over 30 years. In his book, Paul masterfully teaches us dozens of life lessons he has learned from his climb from bankruptcy to the top of the insurance profession by adhering to his core values, always looking out for his clients' best interests, and developing efficient and effective habits in all phases of his personal and professional life. Paul shows us what one can accomplish with a positive attitude, an open mind, a great product, kindness, and the utmost concern for his clients' welfare. He has provided security and well-being for thousands of families and, along way, built an exemplary legacy in the way he lives his life. What a valuable guide for young people beginning their

career and for others, midway through, who want to get back on the right track!"
— Peter Weil, Managing Partner at Glaser Weil Law Firm, Chairman of the Board of the Skirball Cultural Center

"I've known Paul for more than 40 years. I was lucky enough to meet him early in my career, and he's the only insurance guy I've ever had! He made a point to meet with me once a year to review my medical practice goals, as well as my personal ones, to determine if my needs had changed. He always came well prepared to every meeting. He made it his business to know and understand my situation so that he could offer suggestions on how to move forward. You could tell he really cared about the outcome. These yearly meetings were never the kind of dreaded insurance meetings you might imagine. My wife and I enjoyed our visits with Paul immensely. He is incredibly competent and knowledgeable about insurance, but also extremely bright, funny, charming, and the eternal optimist…and he's one of the best storytellers I know! He's a shining example of a consummate professional who really knows how to connect."
— George Weinberger, MD, FACOG

"I feel most fortunate to have met Paul 30 years ago. His knowledge and expertise have been of great significance in my lifetime.

"He has been a great friend and an outstanding assistant in planning my estate and monitoring my specific goals.

"Here in his book, he openly and honestly describes his life and his thoughts, and teaches his successful techniques. Paul is truly a 'relationship guy'—he has much to say here in a most riveting manner."
— Stephen Loeb, PharmD

THE
SUCCESS
CODE

A GUIDE FOR ACHIEVING YOUR
PERSONAL BEST IN BUSINESS AND LIFE

PAUL G. KRASNOW
WITH MONA DE VESTEL

In 1956, I became the luckiest man in the world. I met a woman who not only became the guiding light and principle in my life, but she also became my rudder, navigating me through both good and bad times. She shaped me in every way. I wish everyone the exact same luck as I had. I dedicate this book to my wife, Joyce.

TABLE OF CONTENTS

Acknowledgments

I have been so fortunate to have people who love me and who have pushed me beyond my expectations. First, thank you to my wife, Joyce, who always believed in me, regardless of our circumstances. She is a true Renaissance woman; the world is a better place because of her. Thank you to my dear departed friend Hershey Eisenberg who showed me a new life path. Thank you to Toba Weinstock who joined my team as my assistant for 37 years and 8 months in June of 1977. What a journey we have shared. Last, but certainly not least, a big thank you to my children without whose help and encouragement my life would have taken a different course. They tolerated their father and sometimes even laughed at his attempt at humor.

Prologue

Can You Meet All of Your Needs?

As I sit here today in my home overlooking the Rocky Mountains, relishing in the professional and financial successes of my life, I can remember a time when I wasn't sure how I would provide for my family. In spite of the tremendous level of attainment I have reached, I have not always been successful. Struggling is not merely a concept I have read about in books but something I experienced for many years. This book is the story of how I transformed my life from financial insecurity to building significant wealth. In these pages, you will find the lessons I learned along the way to building a successful career and becoming a whole person.

Summits Have Room for Only a Select Few

Living part of the year perched up in the Rocky Mountains, I've spent a lot of time examining the awesome Gore and New York Mountain Ranges. If you look at those summits, there is not a lot of room at the top. Mount Everest is 29,028 feet from sea level. The ascent takes time and, in fact, not all who attempt to climb make it. But for those who do, they will tell you that the summit is a tiny spot with enough room for only a select few. Going from bankruptcy to the level of success I have achieved could be compared to climbing

Mount Everest. It's not easy, but with diligent and consistent preparation, hard work, and a little luck, it can be done. As my lovely wife coined the phrase in one of her talks: *In order to make it to the top, start climbing! You too can climb a mountain.*

What is the measure of success? What constitutes having "made it"? Surely it can't mean having achieved only financial and material gain. The complex answer to this question requires the examination of the many layers of your life and all of the ways you strive to achieve fulfillment.

Psychologist Abraham Maslow developed his now famous theory of human motivation, "The Hierarchy of Needs," in which he outlines the hierarchical structure of the true definition of success. I have used this pyramid structure to make sense of how I recovered from bankruptcy, by way of transforming the five areas of my life, including:

1. Physiological needs
2. Safety
3. Love and belonging
4. Self-esteem
5. Self-actualization

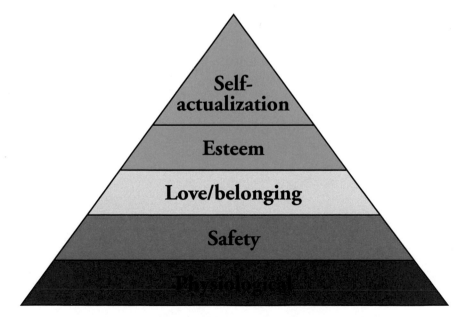

Maslow's lens for understanding human nature and how we move through our lives in search of success sheds light on how we come to prioritize our needs and what we choose to achieve. The first level of needs is focused on obtaining food, water, and shelter. If you can't feed yourself, if you're thirsty, if you don't know where you will rest your head at night, then nothing else matters—you won't be thinking about that vacation trip to French Polynesia or ways of realizing your dream of becoming a famous basketball player. If you're hungry, you will think about ways to feed yourself and your family, and nothing else will be able to enter your mind.

When I look back on my life, I can say without a doubt that I have achieved success. Along my journey, I have gone through every single type of need on Maslow's pyramid—I have struggled for basic needs; I have been held at gunpoint and faced absolute fear and lack of safety; I have fumbled my way through finding balance between work and family; I have grappled with self-esteem, developing self-confidence, and have reached the summits of self-actualization. I agree with Maslow that you first need to meet your basic survival needs before you can achieve self-actualization, but this doesn't mean that you can't work towards fulfillment every step along the way.

According to Austrian psychiatrist and Holocaust survivor Viktor Frankl, author of the famous book *Man's Search for Meaning*, we all have the innate ability to find meaning, even in the most harrowing of circumstances. It is our sense of hope and the meaning we derive from our lives that allow us to not only live beyond the hardships but to find meaning in every moment of our existence.

Why You Should Read This Book: The Push-up Principle

I was talking to a friend of mine the other day and I told him, "Everyone can be number one."

"What do you mean everyone can be number one?" He asked.

PART ONE

Providing Food & Shelter

Nobody can afford to go bankrupt but I REALLY couldn't afford it. My oldest son was only twelve, my youngest boy was ten, and my little girl was just six years old. How was I going to support them?

CHAPTER ONE

Losing It All

I *was terrified. My desperation taught me to never, ever repeat the same mistakes I had made during those 12 years when I owned my four clothing stores. This rock bottom experience was the reawakening that I desperately needed. Seemingly overnight, I awoke to the realization that I had been a foolish man. Losing everything led me to a new beginning of a harder and smarter work ethic.*

In the summer of 1974, my wife, Joyce, and I are woken at dawn by someone pounding on the front door of our home. Terrified, we jump out of bed and run to the front door. Standing before us are two uniformed sheriffs.

"Mr. Krasnow?" One of them asks.

"Yes," I answer, holding the door open.

"You've defaulted on your clothing store lease and we're here to repossess your cars."

It turns out that my landlord in Culver City wanted to make changes to the shopping center where one of the four stores I owned was located. And he was hell-bent on removing all of the small tenants out of there, making it very hard for any of us to do business. Overnight, he took away the outdoor restaurant seating, thereby cutting customer traffic by about 30 percent. This led many of us to leave the shopping center before our leases were up.

The landlord won the judgment against me after I had broken my lease because I found it impossible to do business in that environment.

Joyce and I step out into the driveway where the sheriffs are standing in the crimson light of an L.A. dawn. *How are we going to function without our cars?* I think to myself. As if Joyce could read my mind, I hear her asking the officers:

"How will we go to work if you take the cars? And if we can't go to work, how are we going to support our family?"

This snapshot is one of the low points of my professional life. Here I am, down and out, about to lose the tools that allow us to go to work. My palms are wet and I have a knot in my stomach. I am terrified. I want to find something to say to the officers but all I can think of is the fact that I don't really have the faintest idea of how we are going to go on productively with our lives without our cars. And just when I am thinking that nothing good could come out of this situation, something miraculous happens.

"We've had a lot of dealings with your landlord over the years. He's an extremely litigious man. We'd hate to see you lose your ability to drive to work."

These are the words of the sheriff who pounded on our front door. I can hardly believe it. Joyce and I are not sure why, but miraculously, the officers leave without taking our cars with them. This was a small victory, but to us it was everything. Although it allowed us to continue to drive to work, it didn't save me from having to file for bankruptcy on August 15, 1974.

Reaching the End of the Line

I was 36 and a father of three when I went bankrupt. Talk about being at the bottom of the needs pyramid. How were we all going to survive? Two things can happen to people when they go through bankruptcy: They can either get stuck and become a victim of their own failures, or they can get back up and rally. According to Maslow, only 1 percent of people will reach self-actualization because they don't know how to make it past the first few levels of hierarchical needs such as providing food, shelter, security, and building self-confidence. I could have easily gotten stuck after losing everything. One of the little-known facts about bankruptcy is the terrible shame that it stirs when the newspaper publishes your business's name. This is the moment you have to decide if you're going to allow these external circumstances to define you or if you're going to get back up. I chose the latter.

Like most setbacks, some of the circumstances that led me to lose everything were outside of my control, though some were not. The year before my bankruptcy, in 1973, the energy crisis hit and members of the Organization of the Petroleum Exporting Countries (OPEC) imposed an oil embargo on the U.S.

Overnight, a regulation was put into effect that stated that gas could be purchased only every other day based on your license plate number. People were terrified by the long lines circling around the block for a drop of gas. The mood was somber, and the roads, stores, and malls around the city were ghost towns. Even the smallest thing like putting up Christmas lights in retail stores was no longer possible. Our lives had changed in an instant.

In December of 1972, the year before the energy crisis, my four clothing stores produced $100,000 of business, and in preparation for the following year, I purchased inventory to do $110,000. I was feeling pretty good about the economy until this global energy shock took place. But then the energy crisis hit in 1973. From Thanksgiving until the middle of December my business was down 75 percent. People were very cautious about driving and they were certainly not shopping. Then, around the 15th of December, the holiday rush began—but it was too late. We could not make up half a year's worth of sales in just ten days. It was impossible.

To make matters worse, one of my employees was stealing huge amounts of goods from my stores. The truth is that it was my fault. I was negligent. I was not paying attention. I was running around like a big shot, not taking care of business. Sure, the energy crisis was outside of my control. It was a killer. But I wasn't tending to business; otherwise I would have caught my employee stealing. For weeks, I had suspected something was wrong. I contacted my accountant and told him, "I am making sales but I have no cash flow." He told me not to be concerned. So I sought the advice of a new accountant and told him, "This is what is going on." And he said, "I want you to close on Sunday, and take inventory of all four stores." It took us 20 hours to take inventory, and we discovered that we had 12 percent shrinkage because my employee had stolen over $60,000. In order to make up for that loss, I would have had to sell more than $800,000 worth of clothing. Minding the store had been my responsibility and I had failed. What was I going to do? Fight! That's what I did. I fought to keep the stores open. But it was too late and I lost everything.

Nobody can afford to go bankrupt, but I REALLY couldn't afford it. My oldest son was only twelve, my youngest boy was ten, and my little girl was just six years old. How was I going to support them?

In the days that followed the bankruptcy, my wife, Joyce, went to work for the Stephen S. Wise temple school, working as the transportation supervisor. This petite wife of mine got a Class 2 driver's license so she could be a substitute school bus driver in addition to her main job. Here she was, out there doing it. My wife always figured out a plan. Throughout our 56 years of marriage, Joyce has had so many incarnations, it's unbelievable. She constantly evolves as our lives evolve. I love that about her. I am so lucky to have this woman.

Desperate Times Call for Desperate Measures

After bankruptcy, I filed charges against my employee who had stolen from me. I had gone to court with my accountant who had all of the books proving his guilt. Weeks go by and we are not being called to testify. I call the DA's office where they are overworked and understaffed. "We have not heard anything about our case. Is this normal?" I say to a man's voice on the other end of the line. He puts me on hold and comes back a couple of minutes later. "Your case was dismissed."

"Dismissed! You're kidding! Why?"

"Insufficient evidence."

Unbelievable! Our case had been dismissed because we were never even allowed to testify! A few minutes later, by some crazy coincidence, my former employee's attorney calls to confirm that our case had been tossed out and he added, "We are going to sue you for false arrest." I stay very calm and then I tell him, "I am really glad you're going to do that. Here is what I want you to do. I don't want you to spend your money to serve me papers; tell me when you plan on serving me and I will be here to accept."

"What do you mean?" the attorney asks, sounding confused.

"I don't want you to have to spend money on serving me papers. I'll accept service; it will be done."

"We will certainly do that," he replies.

"Good, because the second I accept service, I am coming down to your office and I am going to blow your fucking brains out."

"Are you threatening me?" he screams into the phone.

I stay very calm. "I am going bankrupt; I have nothing left. I have nothing to live for, so it doesn't make any difference to me."

I never heard from him again.

I was terrified. My desperation taught me to never, ever repeat the same mistakes I had made during those 12 years when I owned my clothing stores. This rock bottom experience was the reawakening that I desperately needed. Seemingly overnight, I awoke to the realization that I had been a foolish man. Losing everything led me to a new beginning of a harder and smarter work ethic.

A week does not go by when I don't think about those early days when I struggled. Even today, whether I am sitting in my house in Colorado or my home on Wilshire Boulevard overlooking the city of Los Angeles, I can still remember the terror of that battle vividly. How did I do it? My journey to success was not an easy road.

Life Lesson Moment

Losing my business and filing for bankruptcy was the rock bottom moment of my life. There comes a time when we are faced with insurmountable odds. Perhaps that moment has already come for you, dear reader. If not, it most likely will. Now is the time for you to ask yourself how you plan on facing this adversity. What are you going to do when the challenges come your way? How are you going to react? The answer to that question will determine the crux of your success. The key to your success does not depend on the severity of the adversity you face but on your ability to get back up.

When facing a huge setback, there is nothing wrong with pausing to take a breath and absorb first the shock of the event, but most importantly the lessons of how things could have been done differently. Even if the setback is outside of your control, there are proactive steps that you can take in order to get back on your feet. And lastly, dear reader, do not let the inertia of this challenge paralyze you. If you allow yourself to learn from this experience and to keep moving, you will look back on this moment with a fondness and a pride for the warrior that you are. Onward, dear reader. Onward!

How to Make a Comeback After a Major Loss, Failure, Setback, or Low Point

Admit it, you're facing failure. It could be a relationship crisis, the loss of a job, being outsourced, or facing bankruptcy. It's time for you to stare the devil in the face and mourn your losses. Deal with those feelings of shame, low self-esteem, anger, and fear and go into battle! Desperate times call for desperate measures. Fight like your life depends on it, because it does!

Action Steps

Name the challenges you're facing. Write down the obstacles you feel are in your way. Is it the loss of a job or have relationships also been damaged? Are you lacking self-confidence or do you need a loan to launch your new idea? Write down every obstacle in the way of your creating the career you want. Discuss your list with trusted friends. Write a matching action or solution for each obstacle. Example: "I need a small loan. Solution: Start a crowd funding campaign to raise the funds." Tackle at least one element on your list each day, until you're done.

Mourn your losses. After a failure, it's normal to feel everything all at once: shame, guilt, low self-esteem, sadness, and anger. But if you can't identify these feelings, you won't be able to deal with them in a healthy way; you'll just know you feel terrible and will stay stuck there. So name those unpleasant emotions and face them. The sooner you claim what you're feeling, the faster you can move on. Cry, vent to a friend, see a therapist, write a letter to your failure, take up boxing or skydiving and scream all the way down. Whatever you do, face those feelings head-on. Sweeping all of these emotions under the rug will only stink up the place. Get cracking now!

Figure out your core values. Your core values are the beliefs and values by which you live. They help you remember what you stand for, so that when you are challenged you'll have a code to stand by in business and in your personal life. Remembering your core values will also help you regain your footing after a loss or failure. To identify your core values, brainstorm about the beliefs and rules that really matter to you. You may find yourself using words like *loyalty, honesty, determination, hard work, striving,* or *integrity.* Keep sharpening your values until you have truly identified exactly what you believe in.

Do not allow external circumstances to define you. Remember that you are not defined by the things that happen to you in work or in your personal life. It doesn't matter if you lose your business or become the richest entrepreneur on the planet; your being, your core values, and your worth remain the same. Take a moment to write a letter to your true self and answer the following question in this letter: "Who am I if I am not a (INSERT YOUR LABELS HERE)?" After my bankruptcy, I had to find my way back from: "Who am I really if I am not a retail business owner?" Find yourself beyond your labels.

Take responsibility for where you are today. I don't care how tough you had it as a kid or whatever calamity you lived through in the past; you're the only one responsible for where you are today. Don't beat yourself up for falling down, but do write down *what,* and more importantly, *how* you could have done things differently. When I faced bankruptcy as a retailer, I wish I realized sooner that I needed to differentiate myself from my competition. What are the things you would do differently the next time you face a similar challenge?

Don't be a victim. After a setback or failure, face whatever happened to you, accept it, and start planning your next move. Wallowing in self-pity only hurts you and delays your progress. Refuse to play the "victim card." If you've done something wrong, apologize.

Sometimes your own failure damages other people. If you have let others down, made mistakes that hurt your friends or colleagues, or have behaved in ways you're not proud of, apologize right away and make it heartfelt.

Get back to your normal routine (and do it better than ever). When you lose control over a portion of your life, it's important to focus on what you can control to regain a sense of normalcy. Start paying close attention to your daily routines, and vigilantly take care of yourself. Get some exercise; eat healthy food that gives you plenty of energy and brain power. Take care to dress well and groom yourself. Clean up your house. Get some fresh air and sunlight. Keeping busy and not letting yourself go will help you really feel your resiliency. If it's something that is rather public, you might be tempted to go underground, but don't let that happen.

Take action on a new passion project. This is the time to sink your teeth into something new and exciting. Start developing a new skill or hobby. Not only will it distract you, but it will give you a sense that new opportunities are on the horizon all the time.

Stop the negative self-talk. Don't say anything to yourself that you wouldn't say to a good friend or to your child. Talking down to yourself by saying things like, "You're so stupid," or, "You'll never amount to anything," does nothing to help you. It only makes the road ahead harder. Instead, develop a set of "positive talk" phrases that reflect back to you the existing strengths of your business. When I was facing bankruptcy, I told myself, "This could be the best thing that has ever happened to me. I will never make the same mistakes again."

Remember your "wins." If you're feeling particularly stuck, remind yourself of the victories you've achieved. Everyone has accomplished something they can be proud of. This is the time to acknowledge those peaks and remind yourself that there are more in store. Make a list of your recent wins and display them prominently in your office so you can see them every day.

Surround yourself with your champions. This is the time to be around people who really care about you and have your best interests at heart. Reach out to beloved family members and friends who love and respect you. They will remind you of your worth. Make a list of the champions in your life and reach out to them on a regular basis.

Keep in mind that failure is part of life. Any successful person has failed and failed often. Keep in mind that failing is just a signal that you need to try again. The only real failure is giving up. Think of the top three failures of your life and jot down the "gifts" or lessons learned from each one.

CHAPTER TWO

Modest Beginnings

I was the hero of my story, the captain of my ship battling the storm. Maybe I imagined I was a hero because I had never been one. But in those days, riding my bike, tossing papers onto my customers' doorsteps, I was free. I never forgot that feeling, and being free is the feeling I love most about my extraordinary success.

In 1949—the year I turned 11—I landed my first job delivering newspapers. I remember the strong gale of the rainstorm that hit Los Angeles that year. After many months of complete drought, a storm broke out bringing 22 straight hours of a torrential downpour onto the City of Angels. As the saying goes, Los Angeles gets only 14 inches of rain a year; you should have been there that day.

The memory of that downpour is still vivid today. Everyone was barricaded inside their homes with their lights on, while outside I pedaled furiously against the raging storm. As I rode for hours drenched to the bone, I would look inside the warm glow of lit windows and wish I were looking out into the world, instead of in. In my 11-year-old imagination, I was the hero of my story, the captain of my ship battling the storm. Maybe I imagined I was a hero because I had never been one. But in those days, riding my bike, tossing papers onto my customers' doorsteps, I was free. I never forgot that feeling, and being free is the feeling I love most about my extraordinary success.

On my paper route, there was a housebound elderly man who lived across from the American Legion Hall. I'd bring him the paper every day and stop by for a minute so we could talk. I don't actually recall the conversations my 11-year-old self had with this man, decades older than me. But I suspect it had to do with the types of things that always fascinated me, like history and the complex mechanisms of the way things worked in the world, back in 1949.

My childhood was a time of change. World War II had just ended and everything was moving quickly. People were still discovering the horrors of the Holocaust. Maybe this old man I visited every day and I talked about how the Soviets had just tested their first atomic bomb. Or maybe we talked about the new invention of the color television. Whatever words we exchanged left me feeling connected and a little less lonely. It was Maya Angelou who said:

"People will forget what you said, people will forget what you did, but people will never forget how you made them feel."

I never did forget how free I felt in those days of my first job. It was not the money that drove me to work; it was freedom. Freedom and the notion that this is what was expected of me. I worked because everyone worked. I did not have a consciousness of earning money. I just knew this: If you had money, you had options, and having options meant you could buy more than one piece of Fleer's Dubble Bubble gum. How can I forget the one piece of gum my brother and I bought together on the black market during the war for a dime and took turns chewing for a month? Not only was Fleer's Dubble Bubble delicious and chewy, but it made the biggest bubbles ever. I'd read the free comics and fortunes on the wrapper over and over again until the paper was soft and worn and you could barely read the words of the characters. Each night before going to bed, my brother and I would put this top-of-the-line piece of gum that we shared into a glass of water to save it for the next day. This stepping-stone experience taught me patience and perseverance in working hard for what you want.

I was born on May 9, 1938, in the neighborhood of West Adams, where most of the affluent families had already moved out by 1910. *Our* West Adams belonged to working class families like my parents who tried to make ends meet. Even though my father later on ended up working as an artist for MGM Studios, my life growing up in L.A. was completely removed from the glamour of the silver screen. My father and my uncles were in the army in World War II. My mother was ill from complications of rheumatic heart fever she had contracted as a child. Due to her extremely poor health, my father was discharged from the army where he camouflaged planes and large guns by painting backdrops. He later worked for MGM as an artist.

My father had bought a small house for $2,500 where we lived our lives on the heels of the Great Depression. We were one of the very few Jewish families in a primarily Gentile neighborhood. One day, I told my mom that I wanted a Christmas tree. It wasn't that I wanted to be a Christian or that I was not proud of being Jewish, but I was tired of being bullied and teased for being different. I was tired of feeling isolated.

Money was a rare commodity in my family. My brother and I were left alone a lot, while my father was attempting to make a living and my mother was struggling with severe health problems.

Do What You Love, Love What You Do

Today, I tell everyone I meet to *do what you love, love what you do*. Of course, being able to do that usually takes place in the culmination of self-actualization, meaning that it is a very rare occurrence. But even when I was 11 years old, and without even knowing it, I was seeking a job that allowed me to be who I am: a relationship guy. Every job I had, with the exception of one, allowed me to chat with people while working. It has taken me many years to realize what I love most about my career, and even some of my earlier jobs like delivering newspapers. They all allowed me to build relationships with people. Building relationships is the cornerstone of my success.

So there I was. I had my paper route. You can have a paper route only when you deliver papers to people who buy the paper. *Peter Piper picked a pack of pickled peppers.* Right? So once a week, I'd knock on doors and solicit new customers. And then once a month, I'd collect the money and get paid.

I delivered papers until I was 13 and was able to get a paper corner. Having a paper corner allowed me to make money when I was not even there. Isn't that the American Dream?

There I was at 13 on the corner of Olympic Boulevard and Doheny Drive. I'd stand in the street and hawk papers. People would drive by and buy them from me. But there are four corners. I could not be on all four corners at once. So I set up a crate with a stack of papers and a cigar box where people would toss a nickel for their purchase. I was in fat city.

That was my afterschool job. I have no idea what my parents were thinking because no kid should have to do this. But on Saturday nights, I worked from 8 p.m. until 3 a.m. on the corner of Sepulveda and Washington Boulevard where I sold the *Herald Examiner.*

I adored my mother—she was the best—but what was she thinking letting her baby boy sell newspapers until 3 a.m.?

While I was in high school, I worked as a delivery and stock boy at a grocery store. Those early days of work were not easy, but I never lost my sense of humor. My boss was an elderly guy. Well, I was 16 years old, so he was probably not a day over 45, but in those days, that seemed ancient. This guy's favorite pastime was to scream questions at me throughout the day. On one particular day, I heard him from the other side of the store hollering, "Paul, where are you? What are you doing?" In those days, I regularly watched a great TV show called *Mister Peepers* with Wally Cox who played a schoolteacher by the same name as the show. Peepers was an odd, mild-mannered man. In one of the episodes, a coworker says to him, "We're going to dinner; come with us." To which Mr. Peepers answered, "I can't; I am counting the chalk." So when I heard my boss asking me what I was doing, I promptly answered, "I am counting the eggs!" No matter how hard things got in my life, I never lost my sense of humor.

After I graduated from high school, I went to Los Angeles City College. That first summer after my freshman year, I went to work at the ice cream plant for the Carnation Company. On occasion, I was asked to fill these five-gallon tubs of ice cream by holding each bucket under a pipe. Sounds easy? Well, it wasn't. Have you ever seen the "Job Switching" episode of *I Love Lucy*? If you've seen that episode, you will get a good sense of my job at the factory.

One day, my supervisor is going to lunch.

"Hey, Paul, can you fill up the five-gallon tub?" he asks me.

"Sure thing!"

He comes over and stands next to me while sherbet flows out of the pipes freely into empty tubs. I had never done sherbet before, only ice cream.

"So make sure you go a little over each time," he says to me grabbing a scraper and smoothing the excess into the next empty tub.

"You got it?"

I get ready to fill up the first tub. That day they're running pineapple sherbet. I am wearing my rubber boots and my rubber suit. And bam! The sherbet comes out like jet fuel.

"Whoa, this is really coming out fast," I tell my supervisor.

"It's nothing," he says. "You'll get it."

Now comes my turn. Before I even have time to scrape off the excess sherbet into the next tub and put the lid on it, the next one is almost full.

"It's really coming out fast," I say to my supervisor.

"Don't worry about it," he says, leaving me alone.

Pineapple sherbet is shooting out all over the place. What does he care? He wants to go eat.

Right off the bat, I have to move the next tub ahead, while the other one is filling. I must look like some crazy automaton moving in fast forward. Before I can get the top on the tub, the next one is full.

I am not exaggerating; within ten minutes there were about 50 tubs around me. I am knee-deep in pineapple sherbet.

"Hello?" I yell. "Can someone come help me?" There wasn't a single soul in the plant but me. What was I going to do? You can't shut the line down because the pipes will freeze. By the time the supervisor came back, I was covered in pineapple sherbet head to toe.

In retrospect, the reason I disliked this job was because I could not build a relationship with an ice cream tub. This type of work did not allow me to be who I am and connect with people. One thing my years of success taught me is this: Do what you love, love what you do. Otherwise you might end up buried in pineapple sherbet.

Those years of constant work, from age 11 onward, set the tone for the rest of my life. I always worked. A worker was who I was. I never wasted a moment. I was always productive. As I matured, I realized that productivity gave me independence. I didn't have to go to my parents for an allowance—not that I would have gotten one. This taught me how to be self-reliant.

One day, lunching with my two friends Bob and Jack, I realized there are different types of people, those like me who always worked and those whose parents cushioned them with their financial support. My friends and I began talking about our childhoods, and from the moment the conversation began, Jack and I just took off talking, leaving Bob out of the loop. The thing is that Bob could not relate to the world Jack and I were describing—a world where we were constantly hustling, constantly working, constantly figuring out ways to be self-reliant. Bob never had a job growing up. He was raised in an affluent family that provided every little thing for him, so he just sat there, listening to our conversation, unable to offer a single word or anecdote.

Maybe it is this rigorous work ethic that also led me to dreaming about adventures. How do you know you're working, if you don't spend some of your time also playing, right? When I was 18 years old I dreamed of traveling the world. I wanted to see and do everything. One day, I approached my father and said to him:

"Dad, I want to see the world. I would like to go to a foreign country and see how other people live."

"Go to Boyle Heights," he answered me, completely seriously. My father was talking about the predominantly Mexican American neighborhood of East Los Angeles. By then, I'd learned that if I wanted something, I had to go out there and earn it myself. What the heck is wrong with that?

Life Lesson Moment

Dear reader, as you embark on uncovering the real you and finding out what you really love, you must go all the way back to your childhood. What made you feel whole in those days? What made you feel free? Was it connecting with people? Was it the freedom of riding your bike and feeling like the hero of your own story? Was it making things? Was it fixing broken toys or making the old anew? The child you once were—the child you still are, on some level—knows the key to becoming the real you once again. Spend a few moments remembering the things that made you feel happy and free in those days and allow yourself to move a step closer to doing what you love and loving what you do.

Examine and Solidify Your Work Ethic

Developing and maintaining a strong work ethic is the foundation for a successful business. Being smart is helpful, but working efficiently and well is vital. It was Maya Angelou who said, "Nothing will work unless you do!" The basis of all productive work is good habits. Here are a few habits that make efficient work easier and more fruitful.

Action Steps

Examine your work ethic. Whether you inherited a healthy work ethic from your parents or you need to build your own, what is your work ethic? Get clear about how you want to work and how well. Write down ten work ethic qualities that you admire and would like to emulate. For example: be punctual, have integrity, be professional, etc. Choose to align yourself and your team with this clearly defined approach to work on a daily basis.

Create and manage a solid schedule. Take time to define the most efficient schedule for yourself and your team. Write down if and when you want to hold recurring meetings. What is the best way for you to get the most productive work done? Stick to the schedule you have established and examine it on a regular basis to see if it can be improved.

Be punctual. This is a simple one but it is essential. Develop the habit of being on time or early for all appointments. People notice. Leave 15 minutes before you think you should, and if you arrive early, use the time to return important phone calls or to ground yourself so that you can approach all of your appointments and meetings with clarity and sharp focus.

Be professional. Manage every interaction with integrity. Don't gossip and be respectful of others. It's not important to be "right." Always remain courteous. Take the time to define your own key qualities of professionalism and live and work by them.

Cultivate self-discipline. Stick to what you set out to do. Make sure that your daily, weekly, and monthly tasks remain in alignment with your short- and long-term goals. Refer to the end of Chapter 4 for more action steps on setting goals.

Get things right the first time. Not only will it impress clients but it's a huge time saver. Take a moment to write down your victories along the way so that you can replicate them. Incorporate these victories and the times when you "got things right" during your team meetings. This approach will help you develop the polished habits of creating success in your business and your life, time and time again.

Never waste a moment; remain productive. It's not about working hard, but about working efficiently. Ensure that your time is never wasted. Productivity is the key to independence. Examine one of your typical weeks and identify the ways you might be wasting time or not being as productive as you could be. Always incorporate process improvement in your team meetings so that efficiency remains one of your points of focus.

CHAPTER THREE

Who Would You Like to Be?

*T*he hand that reaches out to help you is only as effective as your desire to reach out and grab it. You can't do it alone. You can't shake hands with yourself. And that's just a fact.

Facing the Truth

Creating the life you want requires you to become who you would like to be. This means becoming the real you, not just the person everyone else expects you to be. Sadly, millions of humans on this planet go off to work each day dreading their job. The only way to remedy this tragic reality is by going back to basics and listening to your inner self. You can reinvent your life.

There's an opportune moment in life when you're falling into that REM sleep and drifting off to a wonderful dream world—this sweet moment when you're in your heart of hearts, and if you're focused, and if you're introspective, you can see yourself honestly in all of your flawed glory. This is the moment when you say, "Enough is enough!" and, "I'm starting anew."

How Many Psychiatrists Does It Take to Change a Light Bulb?

The wonderful book *Unbroken* by Laura Hillenbrand depicts the incredible story of Louis Zamperini, a flawed man who faces harrowing circumstances during World War II. Suffering from post-traumatic stress disorder, Zamperini lives his mid-life as an abusive drunk, but he doesn't just settle on being a broken man. Instead, through resilience and the desire to overcome insurmountable odds, he opens himself to the possibility of change. His wife takes him downtown to see a young evangelical preacher in a tent and Zamperini's life changes in an instant. The speaker was the American Christian evangelist Billy Graham, ordained minister in the Southern Baptist tradition. Upon first glance, some might think that Zamperini's change came from his encounter with Billy Graham, and in part, it did—but the true catalyst happened within Zamperini himself. Billy Graham and every guru and spiritual leader of the world could not have done a thing unless Zamperini himself *wanted* to change. Do you know that joke that says: *How many psychiatrists does it take to change a light bulb? One, provided that the light bulb wants to change.*

Rising Above Circumstance

Clearly, if you're reading this book, you want to succeed. Some of you might know that you need to make a change but you might be thinking: *The odds are stacked against me. I'll never make it.* Or again: *I don't have the right skills or the right tools on my side.* I am here to tell you that I was the first person to have the odds stacked against me. Growing up, my parents were not sitting next to me coaxing me on how to succeed. They were busy surviving, and I was off fending for myself. The first thing I'll tell you is that you are going to have to craft your own vision of motivation and courage and put your right foot in front of your left and start moving forward. The reality is that there is nothing I can say or do to make you successful, unless you believe in yourself.

None of us, no matter how skilled or polished we become, can build an empire alone. The hand that reaches out to help you is only as effective as your desire to reach out and grab it. We all need a helping hand at one point or another in our lives. But this helping hand is of no value if we are not willing to accept it. You can't do it alone. You can't shake hands with yourself. And that's just a fact.

Discovering Your Hidden Skills

When I started out in my adult life, I had no identifiable skills. None. Zip. Nada.

My friend Marty, who was trained as an accountant, needed a job. He had been the in-house staff accountant for *Miami Vice* and he overstepped his boundaries and was fired. My friends Morry and Stan were sitting with us in my kitchen, attempting to help Marty find a job by looking at the want ads in the Sunday *Los Angeles Times*. While perusing the paper, it dawned on me that I had no formal skills. None of us did except Marty, who actually had had a real job as an accountant. The three of us could never have found a job. There was not one thing in the newspaper that I could do. I couldn't build or fix anything. I wasn't very good with my hands. I had no technical skills to speak of.

"Oh, my God, I've got nothing!" I said to my friends. They laughed, but they knew it was true. It wasn't that I didn't have skills but rather that I had not yet uncovered them. And the skills I did have did not seem to be marketable in any way that I could yet see at the time.

Marty got a job as an accountant. Marty had marketable skills.

One thing I know for sure is that I am really good at thinking on my feet. I guess you could say that this is called being "street smart." If someone throws me a curve ball, I say, "Wow, nobody has ever asked me that question before. Let me write it down and get back to you shortly." This is a better option than blurting out a wrong answer. I also know that later on in life, when I joined the insurance industry, I developed the skill of being able to paint a picture of the life my prospective client would like to have and enjoy. My skills are to give people peace of mind and to make them feel secure. How do I do that? I ask penetrating questions and I listen to what they have to say. What I have discovered in life is that most of us are not listened to. Listening and paying attention and caring what the person is conveying to you is the most important part of establishing a relationship. There is no way that you can create a bond for a lifelong connection without that individual knowing that you truly, honestly and actually care about their life.

I discovered when I joined the insurance industry that I have the ability to ask probing questions, enabling my clients to paint a picture of what they want in the future.

As a salesperson, my job is to make you feel delicious. In the insurance business, I am providing you with a contract that will give you financial peace of mind. I am also giving you a vision of how your financial life will be. Regardless of the business you're in, you want to make your clients feel like they're on top of the world after you've worked with them. Whatever skills you may or may not possess, it's important to move forward. Now the time has come for you to go out and create your own vision.

Most people have developed the terrible habit of listening to the first three words out of someone's mouth and then formulating a reply without listening to the rest. When I work with a client, I turn off my phone and avoid any interruptions from preventing me to really listen. When my clients begin to share their needs and vision for the future with me, there is nothing more vital than that connection. The key is to make your client feel like they are the most important person in the world.

The Sotomayors of the World

One of my great heroes is Associate Justice Sonia Maria Sotomayor, an associate justice of the Supreme Court of the United States. Why do I admire her? Because she was raised in an impoverished environment in New York, hearing guns going off, and yet she became the brilliant and successful person she is today. She rose above the odds stacked against her. When she was seven years old, she was diagnosed with type 1 diabetes and had to take daily injections. Two years later at the age of nine, her father died, leaving her to be raised by her single mom. By the age of ten, she consciously decided she wanted to move out of her childhood environment and become an attorney. Talk about developing the vision of your childhood and becoming the person you truly desire to be! Sotomayor applied herself daily and worked diligently in school. This entry into education became her ticket out of a challenging set of circumstances. She focused on working hard and graduated summa cum laude from Princeton University and then went on to obtain her JD degree from Yale. Sotomayor credits her time at Princeton as being "life-changing," though being one of very few women and Latinos, she felt like a "visitor landing in an alien country" when she first arrived.[1] This did not stop Sotomayor from thriving in her new environment. Just because you're born under a challenging set of circumstances, it doesn't mean that you should let your past define you and how you're going to live your life.

The bottom line is that if you want to find reasons why you can't move up and change your life, you will find more excuses than there are words in the English language. I had to ask myself when I was 18 years old: *Do I want to stay at Carnation and make pineapple sherbet for the rest of my life?* The answer in my case was "no," and the rest is history (and a whole lot of hard work). Some people prefer to hold

---

1   Ludden, Jennifer and Weeks, Linton (May 26, 2009). "*Sotomayor: 'Always Looking Over My Shoulder'*". NPR. Retrieved August 30, 2009.

on to what they have and what they know, rather than striving for a bigger and better life and facing the unknown. What's wrong with making ice cream sandwiches eight hours a day? You get time-and-a-half for overtime; you have your two-week vacation. There is nothing wrong with that. That's fine. But some of you are going to think, *I want more. How do I get it? How do I move into a different stratosphere?*

Life Lesson Moment

The very first step you must take at this point in your journey towards success is a step towards absolute honesty. This is your opportunity to have the courage to look at your own life without flinching and examine the various ways in which you are deviating from the life and person you always dreamt of becoming. Maybe you wanted to own your own business as a horse trainer but now you're working in a pet store, shelving bags of dog food all day. How did you get here? What steps do you need to take in order to change this reality? This is the kind of honesty that I am requesting of you, that you must request of yourself. Facing the truth about yourself means:

1. Admitting what you really want.
2. Uncovering your hidden skills.
3. Getting up and implementing your life's plan.
4. Drawing up a life plan of what you want to accomplish before the end of your life.

Uncover the Motivation to Change Your Life

You have the ability to change your life, regardless of how dire the circumstances. The key to making a change is to uncover your motivation to do so. Follow these steps and take your life to the next level, now.

Action Steps

Harness your willingness to change. Do you want to catapult your life forward? Taking your life to the next level requires unflinching honesty and the willingness to change. Identify three earth-shattering reasons why you are motivated to change your life today. Now match these reasons with three actions that will let you ride the wave to success.

Uncover your hidden skills. Your hidden skills can become the backbone of your business. What hidden skills do you already possess? Take a moment to brainstorm ten natural skills you enjoy using and already have under your belt. My ability to talk to just about anyone on the planet and my joy of building relationships were two such hidden skills that became the backbone of my successful business.

Identify assets in your network. We all have an untapped existing network of people in our lives. Nobody can reach the summit without assistance. Don't be afraid to ask for help. What are the three areas of your business or project where you could use assistance? Now make a list of the people in your current network who could help in some way. Be as specific as you can. How do you see these specific connections helping you? Are they referring you to new possible clients? Are they possible investors? Take the time to brainstorm in this way to connect your current untapped network of people with possible future opportunities.

Go beyond what you know. Are you willing to rise above your circumstances? Can you describe your clear vision of what you would like your business to accomplish and how you would like your life to be? Now, identify areas of this vision that bring you beyond your comfort zone. Check out the exercise in Chapter 4 to go beyond your comfort zone.

Admit what you really want. Sometimes it can be frightening to admit to ourselves what we really want to bring to fruition. What are three elements of your life and/or business that you would like to manifest? Now debunk the story behind the reason for your fears. We are only as weak as the discouraging stories we tell ourselves. For example: Desire: I want to make $1 million in the next 12 months. Fear: I am afraid I am not good enough or smart enough to generate that much money in such a short period of time. New Story: I possess all of the skills under my belt to make $1 million in the next 12 months.

Draw up a life plan of what you want to accomplish. Before you can begin to bring a vision to life, you have to develop a clear plan for this dream. Take a moment to write up a clear description of the vision you would like to bring to fruition. Can you come up with ten steps that will go into implementing this vision? What are all the actions you need to take in order to bring your dream to life?

CHAPTER FOUR

The Power of Youth

*I*f you're still in the early phases of your adult life, start planning ahead. If you're older, get planning too! It's never too late, until it's too late. You can still plan ahead and take care of yourself and draw up a plan of action.

Go for the Unknown

I met my wife, Joyce, when I was 17 years old and she was 15. We were babies. On our first anniversary of dating, I took her to the Carthay Circle Theatre off of Olympic Boulevard and we saw *Around the World in 80 Days* with David Niven and Cantinflas. What a movie. Afterwards, we went to an Italian restaurant on Sunset and LaBrea called Abruzzi. It's gone now. This was a special treat, because growing up, I never went out to eat because of my family's financial situation. Having so little experience with dining out, neither of us really knew what to order when we sat down. The two of us kept eyeing the menu and hesitating until the waiter finally said to us: "Let me take care of you. I'll bring you something you will like." He came back with a dish—I kid you not—it was the most delicious thing I had ever eaten in my entire life. Do you know what it was? *Lasagna!* I still remember the excitement of that moment, like it was yesterday.

Joyce and I both enjoy discovering new things, and that's what we've been doing together since the first day we met.

Four years after our discovery of lasagna, Joyce and I got married during our Thanksgiving school break when I was 21 years old. Joyce had just turned 19 the previous October. We went to Las Vegas for our honeymoon. We were both so young and had not yet seen much of the world. We picked a German restaurant to celebrate our new union, and they served us another magical deliciousness: *whipped butter*! This tells you how sheltered I'd been up until that point.

Even back in those early years, I knew for some reason that I did not want to eat at Johnny's Joint. I wanted to go to Abruzzi. I wanted to discover new things. I have always been adventurous. I've always had upscale tastes. I don't know why.

Life is an adventure. I like that! It's good. That's why I am not a rice-and-beans type of person. I like eating the truffle omelet instead. When you taste something new for the first time, somebody might say, "Try this; it tastes just like chicken."

But what's the point of having something new, if it tastes just like the thing we have known for our entire life? Why do we have this need to reassure ourselves when discovering something new? Why not go for the new adventure instead? There is no better time to experiment and try new things than when you're young.

Capitalize on Your Youth

Some of you are just starting out in your adult life. You want more than what you're experiencing so far, but you're not sure how to get there. You might be thinking: *I have a vista in front of me, but I can't see beyond my fingertips.* This is a very limited view. If you're in those early years of life, then I say capitalize on your youth. Youth is a privileged passage, when you have one of the greatest assets on your side: time! This is the crucial period when people fall away from each other and divide into two groups: those who really hunker down and build a foundation for their future and those who sit around and will have to backpedal later.

When I look back on those early years in my life when I could not yet identify my own skills, I had one thing going for me: I had an intact sense of humor. If you're young, you probably have one too, and guess what? That's a really great thing! Youth is a time when you're open to new ideas and experiences, mostly because you don't know otherwise, and because everything is new and fresh. It's like the lasagna that I tasted for the first time in my life. It was delicious. This excitement you still have for everything new in your life means that maybe you can roll a little better with the punches when the going gets tough, and at times, it will.

The other thing is that when you're older you say, "I better make this work. I'm running out of time." But when you're young, you're invincible; you're immortal. There is no such thing as mortality when you're young. You feel like a superhero.

I know for a fact that there is only one person at the top of every class. There is only one valedictorian who is going to give the graduation speech. And the other thousands of people are going to be sitting out there and throwing their caps in the air, and hopefully, catching the right one. Most likely you're striving to be at the top of your class. There's only so much room for a small group to make it to the top.

When I was starting out, I was striving to be successful, but I had no idea how to go about doing that. I was 24 years old; what did I know? The only certainty in my life at that point was my desire to launch out on my own and to start my own business.

How I Got Started

When I was a kid, my mother always said to me, "Pauly, I want you to have a better life than we did." I never forgot her words. I wanted to have a much better life than my parents did and not have to struggle so hard. But I did not know how to take the stepping stones to achieving my goals. What I did have in those early years was the knowledge that I wanted a better life for myself. I wanted to have financial success and to experience all of what life has to offer. Ask yourself, do you have those same desires?

At 24, I already had one child, and the funny thing about children is that they have a terrible habit: eating. And not only that, but they want to eat all the time, every day, several times a day in fact. My motivation in those days was to provide a good life for my family. Isn't being a good provider a great motivator to move forward?

When you're young, there are two main sources of motivation: hunger and "the spark." Hunger does not require any explanation. If you have not experienced it first hand, you can certainly imagine it. Hunger is the part in the movie when our hero is wondering how he is going to pay his mortgage on time. That is hunger, while the spark is something a bit more elusive. The spark is what wakes you in the middle of the night with excitement. It's that feeling most children have felt at some point when they're looking forward to getting something they've been dreaming about for eternity. It's the push that propels artists to create and businesspeople to win. Maslow will tell you that the spark rarely appears when you're hungry because the despair of hunger consumes every thought and every action of the person experiencing it.

How Do I Get There?

I was hungry for success. I had a deep desire to make a better life. Most people do not have a clear vision of what this requires. This is why students change their majors often. Once you've moved beyond the "fight or flight" mode and you have a career that you want to realize, then you have the spark.

In rare cases, you can have both hunger and the spark at the same time, like those few young people who already know exactly what they want to do very early on. This was the case of Yo-Yo Ma, the French-born Chinese American cellist and prodigy. Born in Paris, he was introduced to classical music at a very young age. When he was just a toddler, his father gave him violin and viola lessons. By the time he was four, Yo-Yo Ma settled on the cello and began giving recitals shortly after that, performing for presidents Dwight D. Eisenhower and John F. Kennedy. This musical genius is one of the lucky few whose early passion was combined with an absolute clarity of purpose. But most of us fumble around for a while trying to figure out what we are supposed to do with our lives. That was certainly the case for me.

Learn from My Mistakes: Make a Plan

One of the tools you can use in order to keep yourself from getting completely lost on the path of your life is to make a plan. My youth was very unsettled. I had no rudder. I owned a business but I wasn't schooled in the process of being a businessman. I opened a clothing store when I was 24 years old. I had an ego the size of Mount Everest. My picture was on the front page of *Men's Wear Daily*.

I thought that I was a big shot, but that was not true. And the reason why my thinking was distorted is because I didn't have the ability to look beyond the moment. I did not plan ahead. I didn't even plan a year out. Don't make the same mistakes I made. If you're still in the early phases of your adult life, start planning ahead. If you're older, get planning too! It's never too late, until it's too late. You can still plan ahead and take care of yourself and draw up a strategy.

When you're young, you're searching, you're experimenting, and you're seeking. That's planning. You're educating yourself. If you want to be a lawyer, you're continuing your education. If you want to be a doctor, you know that you won't start to earn a living for nearly a decade. Those early years are the biggest planning years there are. During this period, you should be planning every moment of your life.

How I Learned to Make a Plan

The first step to accomplishing something is setting a goal. Each year of my career (with the exception of my 20s), I would make a yearly goal for myself. I highly recommend you do the same. Yearly goals are very important. This is how you make what appears to be impossible become possible. When examining your yearly goals, at first it seems like reaching for the stars. For me, in the insurance business, it was always about acquiring clients and figuring out a way to serve my existing clients well and efficiently. At the beginning of each year, I would determine how much income I wanted to earn. The formula I used to accomplish my income needs was: How many people did I need to see in order for one of them to become a client? That number was always daunting. Then, I broke it down, first monthly. How many people did I have to see in a month to do this? And then I'd break it down weekly. And I'd say: How many people do I need to see in a week, in a day, and all of a sudden that unreachable finish, like of a year's worth of goals, would become something I could do. Suddenly my year became manageable.

When you're starting out in your career, there is no better time to set a path for your financial success. It's much better to begin when you're 28 than when you're 38. That's why there are so many people who didn't consider the consequences of their decisions early on, and are now entering into their second careers. Don't make the mistake of just *getting a job*; instead, build a career. Now they have to backpedal. Don't succumb to the stereotypical ingrate quotient of people who take things for granted. Realize your potential *now* and put it to work starting *today*.

This is what I'd like to say to you, the 28-year-old who is reading my book: If you're 28, don't make the mistakes that I made. What I always wanted to be able to do is to open my head and have people walk around it and say, "Whoa, look at these pitfalls. Whoa, there is a volcano erupting." But it's so hard to learn from somebody else's mistakes because the ego gets in the way. Just because you're young does not mean that you have to make the same errors I did. The time to become more efficient is now.

Invest in Your Future Now

Many years ago, I read in the *Wall Street Journal* about the moment when the women's clothing store The Limited became publically traded. The founder, Leslie Wexner, borrowed $5,000 from the bank and $5,000 from his aunt in 1963 to open his first store. By the time it went public in 1969, The Limited had over $1 million in sales. From $10,000 to $1 million in just six years isn't bad. Start investing in your future now.

Warren Buffett, who is one of the richest men in America, is one of the main shareholders of the company Berkshire Hathaway. Did you know that if you invested $1,000 in Berkshire Hathaway stock back in 1964 when Buffett took over the company and the share cost was just $19, it would be worth more than $11 million today? I am not saying that we can predict these types of opportunities, but what you can do is say, "Look, I want to be different. I want to set myself apart. I don't want to be playing all of these video games or watching those who have a little more vision than I do. I am capable of having that vision. I am capable of taking care of myself. I am capable of doing all of these things. I am capable of planning for my future."

Are You Being Efficient?

If you came up to me and said, "What should I do?" I would never say, "Find the motivation." That would never occur to me. I would say, "Are you working efficiently? Give me your workday schedule. Let me see it; show me."

Once I have examined the use of your time, I would ask you to write down what you would like to achieve. You might say money or beauty. You might say health. You might say any and all of those things. Regardless, I want you to direct your life. I want you to be the captain *and* the rudder of the ship. Be the one who steers and stay on course.

I would say to you, "What do you want to do?"

So if you answered, "I want to have a lot of money," that's admirable. But how are you going to get there? Are you working efficiently?

Most of us are not functioning at our highest level of efficiency. Instead, we are wasting time without even knowing it. One of the things I have learned along the way is to pay attention to where I spend my time. Many people keep postponing getting to work or getting the work done. One of my favorite sayings is that "procrastination is a decision unto itself." It's true. If you continuously procrastinate, you're essentially deciding to squander your most important asset: time. Are you wandering around the office trying to find someone to chat with so that you don't have to start working? If the answer is "yes," ask yourself how important is it for you to build that successful career?

The second thing you can do easily in order to become more efficient is to be truly organized, starting on the evening before your workday. At the end of the day, take some time to write down what you have to do tomorrow. Put away your files. Leave a note for yourself on what you need to do and how you plan on doing it. Each night before leaving the office, all of my files for the next day were in order and ready to be reviewed in the morning. Everything on my desk was resolved. So I could start off my day hitting the ground and running at full stride. I was fully prepared. My schedule was all set up. This level of efficiency will help you ensure that you're operating at your highest level of performance.

The Challenges of Youth

If you're young, I suspect you have a hard time realizing the consequences of your actions. I am not saying this condescendingly. I speak from experience. Like most 20-something-year-olds, you might be having a hard time visualizing the consequences of the things you do today. But the truth is, these consequences are real and they can become very difficult. And just because you're 28 years old doesn't mean that you cannot say to yourself, *What do I want to do when I am 29? What do I want to do when I am 30?* There is nothing wrong with believing things like, *I am omnipotent. I am going to live forever. My mortality is meaningless. I am going to have hair on my head forever. I am going to have this kind of skin forever.* But start thinking about your future for those times when you will no longer have that head full of hair or that very firm skin. Because whether or not you believe these things will ever happen to you, I guarantee you that if you have the privilege of aging, these unpalatable changes in your body and in your outlook are indeed coming.

Time to Experiment: Start New Careers

So, when you're graduating from college, you are either going to depend on Mommy or Daddy or you're going to embark upon a career. Now the advantage that you have of being a person starting out is that you have the opportunity to experiment and have several careers. There is no need to lock yourself into one occupation so early on in life, unless you're one of those lucky people like Yo-Yo Ma born with the knowledge that you want to be a cellist when you grow up. Those people are the exception, not the rule.

This privileged time of your youth is your time to experience new things. But by 30, you should be done with your experimentation and get serious about the career you have finally chosen. By then, you might want to go on to graduate school, although not everybody who gets a degree is meant to be a scholar.

The New Vista of Education

Some people think that the main reason for getting an education in general is to learn to count from 1–10 and beyond. But learning isn't just about developing the skills to count but about seeing all of the options that are available out there. It is about meeting new people, discovering new cultures, and stretching beyond your comfort zone. But most of all, it is about gaining a new vista of the world.

An acquaintance of mine named Dave made a radical decision in 1959 when he looked around and said, "I want a better life. I am not going to Cal State L.A. with my buddy Paul. I am going to the University of Southern California with affluent students with names like 'Beau' and 'Buffy.'" In that moment, Dave made a conscious decision to introduce himself to a new caliber of people. This was a pivotal moment for someone like Dave, who came from Boyle Heights. Remember Boyle Heights? The place my father suggested I visit if I wanted to travel overseas? By hook and crook, Dave worked to put himself through USC. And just like that, he gave himself a new vista on the world.

Trust me, it wasn't easy because his family had limited resources, yet somehow he worked hard, and, through his connections made at the university, he became an enormously successful property and casualty agent. He had a very nice office down on Wilshire Boulevard near Western Avenue. And how did that happen? He went to USC not just to get an education, but to gain access to a whole new world of contacts and networks. This is the power of education. When I was at Cal State L.A. in 1961, you didn't make much in the way of contacts.

If you go to UCLA, you get a different perspective. If you go to MIT or any great engineering or science school, what you are going to do is meet people who are of similar ilk and with whom you share a mindset as well as a network, hopefully for the rest of your lives. It is the Daves of the world, those who want to have a better life and who have the courage to take an enormous risk, both financially and socially. So go forth into this big, beautiful world and discover a new horizon.

Life Lesson Moment

I would like to invite each of you to do for yourself what I do for my clients: Take the palette of your desires, hopes, and dreams and paint the canvas of the life you have always wanted. If you have the benefit of being in the prime of your life, meaning you have not yet reached middle age, then you have the advantage of time on your side. You'd be amazed to see what an extra ten years of focused planning and living can do in the big picture of your life. But even if you're well past youth and well into middle age or beyond, I invite you to do this exercise with me.

Close your eyes and envision your life ten years from now. What do you see? Where do you live? Who or what is around you? What are you wearing, driving, and doing? What kind of work environment are you in? Now that you have caught a glimpse of the vision of your older self, take a piece of paper and write down the goals you would like to accomplish for the next year in order to bring that vision to life. Once you have written down your goals for the year, break them down for the month, week, and day.

You will be amazed at how easy this goal-creation process can be. But most importantly, you will see just how powerful this tool can be at setting your life in motion in the direction of where you would like it to go. When you start planning your life in this manner, a goal as huge and seemingly insurmountable as *get my law degree* can be broken down into individual and digestible goals. Before you know it, you will reach that new vista in your life and move well beyond your own imagination.

Become More Adventurous

Fearlessness is next to godliness. One of the key ingredients to a successful life and business is the ability to be and remain adventurous. Follow these action steps to learn how to push aside your fear of a little uncertainty and turbulence along the way and lead a more adventurous, playful, and passionate life.

Action Steps

Go beyond your comfort zone. Complacency is the enemy of success. Building your dream requires an unflinching ability to stretch yourself beyond your comfort zone and do things that make you cringe. Are there activities or actions that would move your business forward but you dread doing? Put the book down and take one of these proactive, uncomfortable actions right now. Now repeat your bravery again tomorrow and the day after that and so forth. Complete one act of bravery a day for a month and watch your results flourish.

Drive your business with passion. I have told you to capitalize on your youth, but let's face it, not everyone is not in their 20s. Does your advanced age mean that it is too late to bring your vision to life? No! Regardless of your age, capitalize on the passion burning inside of you and visualize what you would like to bring to life. Take the time to daydream about what it feels like to live that life you have always wanted. Now get to work and make sure that your to-do list always matches the dream of your imagination.

Tolerate the "gray zones." Every aspect of our lives is in constant flux. One of the keys to being successful is having what I call *the resiliency factor*, which gives you the ability to sit through the uncertain gray zones of yesterday, forego the crumbs of today, and go for the true jackpot of tomorrow. Identify a handful of actions you can take to create more security for yourself while taking a risk to bring your dreams to life.

Get there from here. In order to get to where you want to go, you need to have a clear set of goals. Write down where you would like to see yourself five years from now. Now scale it back to two years, one year, six months, three months, and this month. For each of these time periods, envision the key steps you need to take in order for this to happen. Brainstorm everything that comes into your mind for these things to happen. Now be more specific and turn these ideas into concrete action steps and goals. Check in with your goals for each time period and make sure you're still on track to accomplishing them. Are there ways you need to correct your course in order to get to where you want to go?

Invest in your future now. If you want to know what adventures await you, look at the seeds you are planting today and where you are investing your energy. What are areas of your business or professional and personal life that need redirecting and revamping? Where, and more importantly how, can you adjust your point of focus so that you can begin to invest in your future now?

Become more efficient. Leading an adventurous life comes with the ability to free up more time by working smarter, not harder. Are there ways that you can leverage your existing tasks and the places where you are investing your energy? The best type of income is passive income. How can you begin making passive income today? Write down the areas of your business where you can harness the power of your already established foundation and find areas of your work that can begin to earn more money on their own today.

Have a sense of humor. Having a sense of humor goes a long way during the dry and turbulent spells you might encounter during your adventures along the way. If you know you're not in the best of situations now, how can you keep your sense of humor, enjoy what there is to enjoy, and learn from the lessons being presented to you while keeping a sense of levity and good laughs?

CHAPTER FIVE

Change or Be Dragged

Some people accept change gracefully while others cannot, and they hold on kicking and screaming. When the flux of change happens, you can either adapt by going with the movement, or you can let yourself be dragged.

Some of you might be beyond the years of your youth and are ready for a second career. You've been around the block and you know that what you're doing now doesn't quite work anymore. You might even be at a point in your life that may have never worked in the first place but somehow you settled into the familiarity of it all. If this is your situation and you're in a job or a career that no longer feels right, then you're ready for a change.

Someone Out There Wants Your Life

Being in the middle years of your life, you are graced and endowed with wisdom that comes with experience. You also have the benefit of being able to build on what you've already accomplished. Each passage in your life is and should be seen as the building block for the subsequent decade. As much as you were getting your footing for building your foundation while you were young, now is the time to pour the concrete and start building. As you get older, you're going to start adding the framing. This construction phase of your life is crucial in establishing a solid base for the years ahead.

Success comes down to competition. While some people are off wasting years by procrastinating, the person next to them is not. The truth is that procrastination is a decision unto itself. If you're putting off your work until tomorrow or the next day, people on the other side of the planet are out there grinding away to build a future. We now live in a global economy. As American journalist Thomas Friedman states in his book *The World Is Flat*, the world has been flattened by changes that have occurred in commerce, such as outsourcing, offshoring, and supply-chaining. Our economies have become level playing fields. We are now competing for work with people in China, India, and other countries. We live in a world where countless people from different countries are waiting for one thing and one thing only: to take our job away.

If you're not willing to work hard, someone else will! More and more, there are millions of people out there who are literally dying to have our lives. They are getting on a raft and crossing oceans and trekking for thousands of miles with no resources simply because the risk of their harrowing journey is nothing compared to the hardship of their daily life at home. When you know that the world population is growing exponentially while resources are shrinking, you better be conscious of the fact that there are people out there working hard to surpass you.

Stay Focused

Now that you've reached your mid years, the time has come to get serious about focusing on your goals. This is the moment to get serious, period. Serious about your life. Serious about your relationships. Serious about finances. Many people in this stage of life take care of others. And most of them do not have a safety net to rescue them. Remember those goals you drew up in the previous chapter? Write them down, pin them to your mirror, look at them daily, and stay focused. The journey ahead is a long-winded one, and the key is to stay focused on the course you've drawn up for yourself.

The best way to describe the importance of staying focused is to think of your life as a journey in a train that travels on a particular track. Each track leads to a specific destination. When I look at my life, and, more specifically, when I look at the success of my career, I know that I have made a point of remaining on the track of my choice without allowing myself to get distracted and switch tracks. Life is full of challenges and may require a stop or two along the way. You can certainly pause before you continue on your travels but make sure that you get back on the track you wanted to travel on in the first place. If you remain focused, you will certainly reach your desired destination.

Wanting More—Pace Yourself

Hopefully you are among those who think early on in their life, *I want more!* What does wanting more look like? It means making a difference between two possible life paths. In the first choice, you're saying, "Okay, I am going to settle. I'll get a job selling Ford Fusions. I am going to work on the assembly line. I am going to be the worker bee in a law firm." But in the second option, you're breaking away from the majority and you're declaring loud and clear, "I want more! I am going to do whatever I have to do to get the job done. I want to climb that ladder to the top."

All careers—whether you're a doctor, a lawyer, a real estate person, or an insurance person—require focus and a steady pace. You have to go to work every day and keep at it. Keep at it. Keep at it. By the time you reach middle age, you're adding the walls and the roof of your life. This is the time for you to do the finishing and become the master of your castle.

Extraordinary creations are not built in a day through occasional bursts of efforts, but rather are crafted over long periods of time with daily, steady tasks. Remember that life is not a sprint but a marathon.

If you're sprinting from place to place, not only will you exhaust yourself, but you will have very little to show for it at the end. As you stay focused and on course with your goals, remember to pace yourself and remain consistent with your day-to-day goals.

Reinventing Yourself after a Second Career

Regardless of your age or how dire the situation you have put yourself in during the last 10 or 20 years of your life, you *can* make changes today in order to prepare for a better future tomorrow. In my own life, the train of my own failure at age 36 was charging at me so fast and furiously that it threatened to run me over. By that point in my life, I had one thing I needed to do and one thing only: reinvent myself. Perhaps like you today, I may not have known exactly how to do that, but I did know this: I needed to move forward, and so I did.

What did moving forward look like for me? It meant sitting down and being honest with myself much like you did in that exercise at the end of Chapter 4. It meant envisioning what I wanted to accomplish in my life. I knew that I did not want to flounder financially anymore. And I knew that I no longer could afford to neglect and ignore my family by being absent from their lives. I made changes. I listened to a friend's advice and launched into the insurance business.

By the time I reached my fourth decade, just four years after starting over, I had rebuilt my life completely and created a brand-new career from scratch. Working in the insurance business was not a job, but the beginning of a new career. More importantly, this was the opportunity I needed to build a new foundation to sustain me for the rest of my life and beyond, for the future generations of my family. You might ask: How did you do that? The first thing I did was to learn from the mistakes I had made in the years before my monumental bankruptcy. I asked myself some tough questions: *How did I get here? What actions did I take to result in this dire reality of the last few years?*

In addition to learning from my mistakes, I also had to figure out a way to become financially smart and draw up clear financial goals for myself and for my family for the years ahead. This required me to be honest with myself and recognize that the demise of my business and my financial failure were entirely my fault. I had to look in the mirror and see that I had gone bankrupt because of my own actions and not because of anyone else's choices or decisions. I faced the fact that the life I was leading was the direct consequence of my own actions. This kind of brutal honesty is not for the faint of heart. Most people do not have the courage to take full responsibility for their life and most importantly for the failures in their wake. But if you muster the courage to sit down and face your own mistakes, you will free yourself up to learn from the painful consequences you are facing today. You will not only give yourself the chance to learn from your mistakes, but you will also begin to trust yourself in knowing that you have the knowledge to create a fiscally sound business.

Building a fiscally sound business is what I did in those early years following bankruptcy, and the biggest lesson that I learned was that I had wasted a lot of time in my life. Realizing this was very painful for me, but it allowed me to let it go and move forward with a lucid mind and a clear intention to fortify my business moving forward. This was the point in my life when I consciously became an excellent businessman.

Sometimes the market undergoes so many changes that it forces you to reinvent yourself. This was the case of an acquaintance of mine who used to work as a wedding photographer until every person in the world began walking around with a high-performance camera on their cell phone. So what did our former wedding photographer have to do? He had to find a new way of earning a living. He began taking pictures of food for restaurants and publications like *Vail-Beaver Creek* magazine. That's innovation! Today, he is so busy that he can barely keep up with the number of clients who request his services. He no longer has to wait for people to put on weddings in order to get new clients. This individual was able to take his skills to the next level and adapt with the changing times. Ultimately, this innovative ability to move forward efficiently with clear vision and a solid strategy is the definition of an excellent businessperson. This man is someone who is willing to work hard every single day, without losing focus of his big-picture goals. Someone who is willing to get his hands dirty in the everyday mundane tasks of hard work. That, my dear reader, is a successful businessperson.

Making a Decision to Move Forward

Some of you are maybe further along in your life path and are facing the desire to make a career change. Perhaps your business slowed down to a complete halt or your first business was a blowout. Or maybe you've been at a job for a long time but have caught that glimpse of truth and clarity in your heart of hearts and know you're now ready to become who you really wish to be. Whatever the case may be, you, too, are ready for a change, and the fact that you're further along in your life should definitely not stop you. It's never too late to reinvent yourself.

My uncles didn't start college until they were 31. Not only did they decide to go to school later in life, but they went for their PhDs! The long educational process took them well into their 40s by the time they attained their degrees. Prior to making this extremely gutsy and risky change, one of them was a cab driver and the other was a milkman. Somehow, later in life, they both reached the point of *enough is enough* and decided that they needed a college education. For some of us, it takes a little longer to find the path to success. We don't all easily find ourselves. That was certainly the case for me.

We all know that change is not the most comfortable part of our lives. Psychologists will tell you that one of the greatest stressors in someone's life is moving to new surroundings. Knowing this sheds light on the fact that changing jobs, or, better yet, building a new career, is also not the most grounding activity. But from the vista of my older years, I will tell you that this process of transformation is a gratifying experience, providing you find the courage to do it. Some people accept change gracefully while others cannot, and hold on kicking and screaming. When change happens, you can either adapt by going with the movement or you can let yourself be dragged.

Embrace New Opportunities

The world is in constant flux. The companies that are flourishing today may go under tomorrow. Ideas change, technologies evolve, and people redirect their interests. If you want to be in business, any business, you're going to have to learn to think on your feet. You have to learn to be nimble and fast and most of all, learn to become flexible. Think about companies such as those in the check-printing businesses. This was a former booming industry that had customers upon customers and needed to transform and reinvent their market or go under. Nowadays, there are more methods of making an electronic payment than ever. Currently, I write only about six checks a month when I used to write dozens.

Look at the Blockbuster Video business. Remember those days when you had to drive to return your video? Every major city had the recognizable blue and yellow logo of that business. Those days are long gone. Today we no longer need to go *out* and rent a video because we can stream it directly onto our various devices and access digital content in a heartbeat for half the price. Even mega corporations aren't safe from the fluctuations of the marketplace. I just bought a Cuisinart juicer from Amazon, including tax and no shipping charge, for $30. Who can compete with that?

You may have to reinvent yourself even if you are a household name like author Judy Blume, originally strictly known for writing young adult books, and who reinvented herself by writing books for the adult fiction market with titles like *Summer Sisters* and *Smart Women*. I admire people who have the courage to reinvent themselves, especially later in life. I reinvent myself all the time. Whether we like it or not, the world is changing and it is up to us to transform with the waves; otherwise, we'll get swallowed. The last thing you want is to become obsolete.

If you were Western Union, the leader in providing telegram services to the world, you're thinking, *Uh oh, no one sends telegrams anymore. What am I going to do?* Then you become the leader in financial and communications services and offer money transfer services instead.

You may have to reinvent yourself. I like the word *reinvent* because it implies that like everything else in the world, you are not predefined and you are not static. You are a person in flux.

Once upon a time, maybe you were a surfer dude with a lack of knowledge of how to bring your dreams of owning your own surfboard store to reality. Now, two decades later, you have gained the vision to see where the world is going and the knowledge of how to bring your dreams to fruition. Now, you've not only opened your own business but you've expanded your surfboard store to include snowboards and skateboards and you're breathing the air of relevancy. The oxygen that you're breathing is the oxygen of today. It is that kind of visionary approach to business that is making you relevant.

I have a friend who used to own four gas stations in Las Vegas. He sold them all because he said that gasoline sales were down by 25 percent and he wasn't making as much profit now that cars are getting better mileage than ever. He was right. My old Ford Explorer was getting 17 miles to the gallon, and my new Lincoln was getting 22. Now I drive a Tesla and I require zero gas. One day in the not-so-distant future, gas stations will become obsolete, and we'll all be driving cars running on alternative fuel sources.

When I look back over the last 40 years, the radical changes that have taken place in business could not have been predicted. The advent of computers has changed the way every industry conducts business. Another major change that has taken place is the sharp focus on customizing client and customer needs.

The quality of service that I provide my clients today has been greatly enhanced by technology over the course of the four decades of my career due to the access of information now available to all of us. When I guide my clients through their financial goals, I am able to design a program based on their needs in just a couple of hours instead of a couple of days. Yet, while I benefit from these many process improvements, I still need to make the appointment and I still need to have a face-to-face meeting. The power of face-to-face interaction cannot be replaced by technology, and yet more and more we rely on technology to do the work once performed by the hands of a human being.

When I recently purchased my Tesla, I learned that these amazing cars are almost entirely built and assembled by robots. The Tesla plant in Freemont, California, needs only 3,500 people to produce cars. Change is evident in every industry.

Don't Try; Just Do It

"Try" is a word I have eliminated from my vocabulary. We've been talking about how to make a change in your life. It's not rocket science. We all have a tendency to make life so complicated when it actually isn't. You're going to change your life for one—and only one—reason, and that is because you want to change. People say they're going to *try* to change. Try? There is no such thing. There's doing it and not doing it. Ultimately, change is brought on by necessity. If you're going to exist in the business climate today, don't say, "I am going to try to change." Either you're going to change and stay competitive, or you're not.

For whatever reason, if you find yourself stagnating without the ability to move forward, there is no shame in asking for help. We are not always able to do things alone. People who go to hear motivational speakers or who pick up a book like the one you're reading now have one thing in common: hope—the hope to make something new happen, transform their lives, and make dreams come true. There are resources out there to help you make the changes necessary. But you must seek them out. You're never going to change your life unless you take the first step. And you can't say, "I am going to try to do this." You either do it or you don't.

There's Only One Curtain Call

Whenever I face difficult challenges in my life, I like to remind myself that it's never too late to change. No matter how dire the situation, there is always a possibility for transformation. After all, you have only one curtain call. On that fateful day in August of 1974, when I reached the end of my rope, if you'd asked me whether or not I would be going on a five-week vacation of a lifetime to celebrate the five decades of my life, I would have hardly believed it. When I turned 50, I wanted to appreciate time and the passage of my life and I rewarded myself with a five-week vacation, one week for each decade. I did it in celebration of the past 15 years of my life and I wanted to share it with my wife. But most importantly, I did it because I wanted to acknowledge how far I'd come, both in the noticeable, external successes and also in the internal growth within myself.

The only real challenge in creating the life you've always wanted is your inability or unwillingness to really free up your imagination to envision your dream in all of its glory. How often do we limit ourselves when envisioning the success we are capable of achieving? When you finally reach the summit, you might realize when you get there that it was merely a molehill hiding the first few steps of the base of a truly magnificent mountain ahead. Don't settle for the limited vista of your present-day life. Instead, allow yourself to be willing to travel well beyond the bounds of the landscapes you may not be able to imagine today.

Our culture tends to idealize the cult of youth, but I am here to tell you nothing can surpass the power of a life well lived and the distilled wisdom of the lessons learned and mistakes faced. What if I told you that the sixth decade of my life was by far the most successful? This was the time when I did the most business. Why is that? Because I had finally reached a point where I was comfortable, truly comfortable, with the person I'd worked so hard to become. Today, as I live out the years in my seventh decade, I am content with the fact that I have become a person of great wisdom.

As you contemplate making a major change in the later years of your life, I want you to remember that the only curtain call is the final one. Until then, it's never too late to change and to keep moving forward. As I write these words, I am reinventing myself. At the end of February 2016, I closed my office after more than four decades. It was a dreadful day. I cried. Closing that chapter in my life was an emotional time that made me feel extremely vulnerable. I was mourning a chapter of my life. My life was not over, but I still needed to mourn a leg of the journey spanning more than 40 fantastic years. With every ending comes a new beginning. And with every beginning comes risk. I am ready to enjoy the next chapter of my life. Are you?

Life Lesson Moment

When you face a setback in your life, you clearly have two choices: Remain stuck or begin to move forward and reinvent yourself. Here you are—book in hand, or maybe you're reading this book on your digital device. You're mustering the courage to look at your own life with that level of absolute honesty. You can see that some of those choices you've made in your life so far are no longer serving you. You might even be realizing that they never served you in the first place. Now is the time for you to forgive yourself for deciding, once upon a time, to walk that unfulfilled path. Maybe choosing the road most traveled was what you thought you needed to do at the time.

Whatever the case may be, forgive yourself. Accept whatever reasons you may have had for the making the choices and decisions that led you here today and simply let them go. The good news is that you are now at this juncture in your life when you have mustered the courage to admit to yourself that you *must* make a change, and must do so *today*. I am here to tell you, that momentum goes a long way and setting yourself in motion is the first step to creating that new life you've always wanted. Now is the time to move forward and travel towards the authentic life waiting for you. Once you let go of the shame and fear attached to those old choices—to that old self—you will feel lighter and freer than you ever have before.

I am certain that this process of letting go will allow you to move into spaces within yourself and within a world that you never knew existed, but subconsciously have always known. When we become our true selves, we become greater and bigger than anything we could have ever imagined.

How to Stay Focused While Dealing with Life's Challenges

Every successful person will tell you that their success depended on their ability to stay focused through the most trying times along the way. Do not allow yourself to be distracted by events and perceived obstacles that may try to convince you to give up. Once you accept that failure is not an option, you can begin to hone your focusing skills and keep your eyes on the prize.

Action Steps

Stay focused—the power of consistency. Rome was not built in a day. Successful people strive for their goals, not in short, inconsistent bursts of energy, but in repeated, consistent efforts. What daily rhythm can you develop right now to begin crossing off your goals? And remember, that consistent passion and enthusiasm are the fuel to pushing through any setbacks along the way.

Stay one step ahead of the game. Seize new opportunities. Are there areas of your business you see emerging with new hidden opportunities? Take some time to identify the underdeveloped areas of your career so that you can begin to take action to bring these opportunities to fruition.

Push past your perceived limitations. We are only as successful as our perceived limitations. Identify the areas where you feel you are challenged or limited and then push beyond that perception. Envision concrete steps you can take to go beyond these points. I like to return to what I call the *push-up principle*. If you believe you can do only five push-ups, do six and so forth. Write down the number of the most money you've ever made. Now increase that number and link it to your concrete goals for the year from Chapter 4. Break these goals into achievable, bite-sized chunks of action steps and you will have your year of milestones cut out for you.

It's never too late to reinvent yourself. During the course of your lifetime, you will be called upon to reinvent yourself, time and time again. Don't let yourself stay stuck in what you know. Make the most of the resilience you now have under your belt with overcoming previous challenges and strive for new horizons. As you envision this new version of yourself, what are some steps you can take today to put that new self into action?

Failure is not an option. When you realize that failure is not an option, it becomes clear that there is no stopping at the first obstacle you encounter along the way. There is an opening, even in the most stubborn of barricades. Where is the opening in your current wall of obstacles? Is there a secret passage you had overlooked but is now emerging in front of you? Take that hidden path and forge ahead. Just keep your eye on where you want to go and you might find that this setback along the way was actually a shortcut to your desired destination!

CHAPTER SIX

Serve Clients; the Money Will Follow

I *f you become my client, you will most likely purchase seven policies from me in your lifetime. I don't focus on the commission. My philosophy on making money, a lot of money, is a simple one: Serve clients, nurture those relationships, and the money will follow.*

Serve Clients

Some people get up every day and think only about how much money they are going to make—they're chasing dollars. There is nothing wrong with making a clear financial plan and setting out to make a certain amount of money each month. In fact, I would suggest you do that very thing. But the last thing you want to do is to lose sight of the clients you're serving and the fact that you should be building a solid client base and not worrying about dollars. Remember, you are in business for the long haul.

If you become my client, you will most likely purchase seven policies from me in your lifetime. I don't focus on the commission. My philosophy on making money, a lot of money, is a simple one: Serve clients, nurture those relationships, and the money will follow.

What do you need if you're 36 years old and have a family? You need income. You *do* need to pay the mortgage and you *do* need to support your family, but trust me—don't think income. Think clients first.

The Value of Success

It took me a few years to really understand the importance of developing clients instead of focusing on dollars. When I was a student, my buddies and I would sit in the bungalows at L.A. City College and dream about being rich. For us, being rich, being at the top of our game, was making $25,000 a year. This was back in 1958, when I was 20 years old, so $25,000 was the equivalent of $205,000 today. That was a lot of money back then, and it is a lot of money now, especially if you're 20 years old and you grew up in your father's house in West Adams. But this was as big a dream as we could come up with in those days. Maybe a better dream would have been to come up with an actual career that I loved, but all I could imagine at that point in my life was making the equivalent of $205,000 a year. Sitting here today, as I write this book in my office in my home overlooking the Los Angeles skyline, I could not have imagined that I'd be living the life that I live, owning a magnificent estate home in Vail, being a member of two country clubs, having traveled all over the world. The reason why I could not have imagined this life is that I did not know this lifestyle existed. You see, back then, we didn't have access to all of the forms of communication that people have today. There was no sitting around and watching reality TV shows about people who don't add anything to the world other than having big boobs, big fannies, and wearing fancy clothes while still managing to make millions of dollars. There was none of that when I was growing up. So my buddies and I could not really see beyond our tiny horizons. Not that seeing those shows broadens your mind to bigger dreams, but it gives you a view on the world you did not know existed.

Growing up in Los Angeles, you see signs of wealth everywhere. My parents would drive by country clubs here in L.A. and admire the ability to belong to such a beautiful place. This was not something I ever imagined I would be able to do myself later on in my life.

Buying a Marc Chagall

Focusing on dollars is kind of like buying art only because of its monetary value, rather than for your love of the art itself. Some people own a whole series of art pieces for investment purposes only. Maybe they bought *Les Noces de Pierrette* by Pablo Picasso for $49 million. Or maybe they bought *Portrait of Doctor Gachet* by Van Gogh for another $82 million. These paintings in private collections today most likely live somewhere in a vault waiting to appreciate and gain in value each year. They probably don't grace the gaze of art aficionados like myself.

I remember when I bought a Marc Chagall. What did I know about Marc Chagall? Did I ever believe that I was an art collector? That I would create a collection like the one we have now? No. You know what I believed? *Gosh, that's a pretty picture.* I liked it. Whenever I'd look at the painting, the experience was pleasing to my senses. At the time of my purchase, we lived in our 2,400-square-foot house in Northridge with green shag carpeting. At the time, it was a stretch for me to buy the painting, but I did it because I loved it. Yes, I had the capital, but I didn't buy anything for a long time after that. You don't have to believe something in order to make it happen, especially if you don't know it's there to be believed in. The reality is that you *can* in fact become something that you did not know you could become.

Over the years, Joyce and I have periodically purchased a piece of art. But because we are not experts, we hired a consultant to make sure that what we were buying was not only of great quality but also that we were not overpaying for it. We became art collectors even though we had never envisioned doing so. It is possible to create something you never envisioned in the first place. Throughout our travels, we gravitated to all of the museums and art galleries. We allowed ourselves to transform and go through this metamorphosis from people who like to look at beautiful art to people who acquire it. This change in us was something that happened progressively. It was a new facet that developed through the years. And then one day it dawned on us what we had become art collectors. The point here is that you can in fact become someone you did not even know you could be.

When I bought that Chagall, I wasn't chasing an investment or chasing dollars. I bought the painting because all I thought when I looked at it was: *Wow, I really love looking at this fabulous piece of art.*

One thing you will discover about me is that I love to enjoy life. I am a *foodie.* I love to eat a good meal, or enjoy a sunset in Paris. I believe that life should not be bypassed but rather that it should be lived, and most importantly, life should be savored. So for me, buying art for the sole sake of investment is not what I do.

Every Company Has a Superstar

One of the most gratifying events in my career was being the number one insurance agent at Northwestern Mutual Life Insurance Company. There is a superstar in every field. I look at people in my company. I look at people in various areas of sales, and there's always somebody who is a standout—a star. For the longest time, I didn't realize it, but guess who was the star? Me! *How could that possibly be?*

Do you know why I became the number one in my company? The answer to that question is in this entire book, but the short of it is this: My goal was always to build my clientele and I was passionate about my work. So passionate, in fact, that Monday was my favorite day of the week. It was Winston Churchill who said:

"The fortunate people in the world—the only really fortunate people in the world, in my mind—are those whose work is also their pleasure."

I was among those fortunate ones. I loved my career so much that I could barely sleep on Sunday nights. I'd look at my calendar and see all of those appointments I had lined up, and couldn't wait to get in there and do right by these clients. Some of you might be thinking that you won't be able to accomplish what I am suggesting because you don't fall in the category of people who love their jobs. In fact, you might fall in the majority of people for whom Sunday night brings on the blues, that doomsday feeling and knot in the pit of your stomach that says, *Oh no, I can't believe the weekend is over already.* But isn't life too short to live only on the weekends? Wouldn't you love to be excited about your life seven days a week? If you fall in that category of people having the blues on Monday, I will tell you this: Make a change and make it NOW. I dedicate an entire chapter of this book to making a change in your life and becoming who you really are.

Go After Your Goal, Not the Money

When the American medical researcher Jonas Salk discovered and developed the polio vaccine in 1955, he made medical history. Up until 1957, polio was considered one of the most terrifying health threats in the world. How did Salk do this? Was Salk pushing to be number one in his field? Most likely not. But he did have the clear goal of eradicating polio—a lofty goal that would certainly benefit the entire human race. So my advice to you is this: Don't seek to be number one in your field. Instead have a clear goal that provides a service or product to clients and go after it with everything you've got. Eradicating polio is a good example of an extraordinary feat that required achieving steps that did not inherently focus on being number one, but resulted in being so in the end.

Certainly, every businessperson can and should have the goal of obtaining more clients and providing them with the finest service and the most superior product.

My objective was always to have new clients. New paying people that I could add to my existing client list. It was futile for me to go after being the number one agent in the company because there were 8,000 agents who were also going after their dream, and I had no control over what they were doing or thinking. All I could do was focus on my own needs and desires since I had no control over what anyone else was doing. Remember to focus on your own side of the fence, keep plugging away towards surpassing your own ever-evolving limitations, and don't waste time worrying about whether or not your neighbor is succeeding.

Being Number One Is Relative

In 1977, I was the leading agent in the company for that year. And then some guy beats me by a hair and he becomes the number one agent in the company. But is this the most important thing? To be number one? As the years progressed, I realized that the most important achievement for me is to be the person I have always strived to become: a hard-working man of integrity respected in his field. A man who is not afraid to show up every day and work towards accomplishing his goals. These qualities have become more important than any large commission. After all, isn't the road to wealth on the way to wholeness?

In every business, there are the rainmakers and the worker bees. One is not more important than the other, but these different types of work do not bring in the same amount of income. Go out and define what it means for you to be number one and then go after it.

You Can Self-Actualize

Let's say you're at the beginning of your career. You went to law school and graduated with decent grades. Shouldn't this be one of the most exciting times in your life? But instead, you feel lost. No matter what you do, you just can't seem to get ahead. In every business, there are highly intelligent and sophisticated people who don't seem able to move up the ladder. Why is that? The biggest reason why people don't succeed is that they don't see themselves as any better than they actually are. Many people think, *This is all I deserve*. Yet they deserve more. But they don't *think* they deserve more. The key is to believe that you have something to offer the world. Because if you don't think that your actions and work will bring value to our planet then you won't do a thing. I have always believed that I had something to offer the world.

In order to believe in yourself, you might need to venture beyond your comfort zone. So many people are not willing to stretch themselves beyond what they know. One of the reasons that I continually created opportunities for myself is that I constantly ventured beyond my comfort zone in order to go after what I wanted. I knew I wanted to buy that Marc Chagall painting; I knew I wanted to live in that special house. I knew I wanted to experience something I had never experienced before. That is what I wanted and that is what I did. You, too, can do the same.

Share the Profit

When I owned my clothing stores, I wanted my employees to have a fair and equitable opportunity to share in the profit. Given that my employees were taking part in building the success of my business, they received a base salary plus 3 percent commission on their sales. When I hire someone or purchase a service, I want everybody to make a profit and to share in the goodness of success. Satisfied employees make for a happy and profitable business.

Develop a Career vs. a Job

There is a big difference between doing a job and building a career for yourself. When you just have a *job* instead of a *career*, you are merely putting in the hours. You are biding your time. This is the difference between enjoying your life seven days a week vs. living only on the weekend. When you wake up and find yourself in a job that you dislike, it's time to make a change. Sometimes the change is a radical one and requires you to go into an entirely new field altogether. Sometimes the change is merely incremental and does not mean you have to leave the company or business that you're in. It might mean negotiating a change in what you are actually doing for that business.

Early on in my career, I decided to research a management position at Northwestern Mutual. In this position, I recruited agents and supervised their work. I had to face it; I was not in my element. I couldn't stand the work. I did it for five years, but it didn't work. What I disliked most was having to supervise these other agents, which really felt like babysitting rather than managing. My income was derived from the agents I was managing. I supplied them with office space, secretarial services, everything they needed to run their business. But the problem was that some of these agents were simply not producing. I don't know what they were doing. One day, I walked into the office of one of the agents who was a guy in his late 30s, a father of three, and saw that he was not working. "For heaven's sake, what are you doing in here? Go to work!" I said to him. That was the straw that broke my back. I had to tell a grown man with children to go to work. I was not cut out to put up with other people slacking on the job. The reality is that if you're in the right field, and you're doing something you love, you're not going to slack. But the bottom line is that if you want to be successful, you are going to have to put in the time and effort. If you're willing to work efficiently at what you're doing, then you're a step closer to success.

Today I realize that I became the star in part because I went after my goal of acquiring clients, not dollars, with complete passion, and

I did it by providing a service that would benefit them and their families for generations to come. I was in the business of improving people's lives. With my services, my clients were prepared to weather the storm. During the recession, I got a lot of calls from clients thanking me because I provided a product for them that was secure and conservative with a relatively risk-free investment component. Every life I touched, I made better.

Life Lesson Moment

Whether you're already building that wonderfully fulfilling career or not, you are most likely contemplating how you plan on serving your current or future clients or customers in order to reach the full potential of your business. But serving clients effectively and authentically requires that you have a full awareness of your core values. Identifying these core values is a fundamental aspect of building that solid base your business requires in order to flourish. Let's take a moment here to clearly identify those core values so that you can ensure they reside at the center of each of the decisions you make in your business and, dare I say, your own life.

When I tell you in this chapter to develop new clients, to nurture those relationships and the money will follow, I am implicitly asking you to ensure that your core values always reside at the heart of each of those client relationships. My core values are simple: integrity, providing security for my clients, and hard work on a daily basis. Recently, I heard author Elizabeth Gilbert talk about Iyanla

Vanzant's definition of integrity as being an alignment of our heart, mind, and voice all saying the same thing.

Every decision I make in my own business comes down to my three core values of integrity, client security, and hard work. Upholding my level of integrity and making sure that my heart, mind, and voice are all saying the same thing is a crucial aspect of how I conduct business. Providing my clients with services that bring them more security and peace of mind also remains a point of focus. And lastly, the cornerstone of my core values is hard work. As you continue to make your way through the pages of this book, you will see that most of life is mundane. I strongly believe that one of the reasons for my success today is my willingness to put in the hours and the hard work on a day-to-day basis. Every time I approach a decision in my business, I make sure that the actions I am about to take are in alignment with these three core values. If they are not, that tells me that the action is not the right one for me and my business.

Take a moment right now to uncover your core values. Find a pen and piece of paper and write down values that are important to you. Write as many of these as they come to you. Don't stop and think too much about it right now. You can go back and make sense of your list later by refining and consolidating the results.

Once you have a solid list of words, go back and see which ones overlap. If you wrote down "compassion" and "kindness," then ask yourself: *How do they differ and what does each one mean to me?* You might have words like "honesty," "kindness," "environment sustainability," "compassion," or "service" on your list. Streamline the list and see if the overlapping concepts can be combined into one all-encompassing value. Once you have a shorter list, jot down a memory associated with each word. Maybe you heard and saw your parents enact these values in their own lives as you were growing up, or maybe you witnessed these in the lives of mentors or people you highly admire. Regardless of their source, core values resonate true when you think about them.

Now look at your list and circle the top three most important values. These will be your anchor core values representing your ethical and emotional focal points when you make a decision in your life. In the beginning, feel free to display the list of these values in a prominent location in your office or home.

Each time you have to make a decision, look at your list and see if that action you are considering taking will in fact conflict in any way with your values. In the end, decisions are either in alignment or in conflict with these. Once you align every incremental decision with your core values, you will ensure that you and your business remain anchored to your true path.

How to Build Better Client Relationships

Building solid client relationships is the cornerstone of any successful business. If you learn to nurture these connections, your business will grow and thrive and take you to horizons you never imagined possible. Whether you are committing to a personal code of integrity, giving your clients peace of mind, or finding ways to show your clients you care, following these action steps will help you solidify your client connections and allow your business to grow exponentially as a result of these nurturing efforts.

Action Steps

Commit to a personal code of integrity. Integrity should be a core value that steers all of your client interactions. This means committing to being honest and working hard with their best interests in mind. Develop a set of business integrity mantras you can strategically place around your office on Post-it notes or even posters and remind yourself to always align all of your decisions with this code of business conduct.

Give them peace of mind. Your clients should always be in good hands with you. Develop a system that works for you to proactively give your clients the highest level of service at all times. Whether it is having a perfectly tweaked project management system in place in your business or having a very clear communication system, make sure you that you respond to your clients in a timely manner and that you provide expert answers to all of their questions.

Always fulfill your promises. If customer connections are the cornerstone of a successful business, trust is the cornerstone of a healthy client relationship. Remember to keep your word and to deliver without fail. Keeping your word can be as small but equally important as never canceling an appointment or going over the allotted time for a meeting. This guideline may seem simplistic, but this approach will not only impress and delight them, but it will allow them to trust you with more business in the future. Building client trust makes you a winner every time.

Be honest about what your services can deliver. Don't oversell or overpromise the results you offer. Manage your clients' expectations so they won't be disappointed. Put them in touch with others who can help them. Expose your clients to your networks just to be helpful. Maybe they come to see you for insurance policies, but your consultant pal from college could help them streamline their business initiatives—so you connect them up! This will only widen your networks and strengthen your client relationships.

Don't sell your customers products they don't need. Be upfront about products that would be a waste of their hard-earned money. Make your client's best interest your focus in approaching clients with your services. This tip is part of a larger philosophy of moving away from seeing a client as an immediate sale and moving towards building a long-term relationship. This approach ensures that you are successful in building a solid foundation for your client relationships.

Deliver consistent service. Clients come to expect what they have experienced with your services in the past. Align yourself with a clearly defined mission, set of goals, and level of commitment and ensure that clients receive the same level of care by delivering consistently high-quality service, time and time again.

Be authentic with clients. Authenticity, by definition, can't be faked. Customers will know if you are being friendly just to make a sale. Genuine interactions allow people into your life by sharing your personality and getting to know the real you. Friendliness goes a long way.

Find thoughtful ways to show you care. Send birthday cards. Make a donation to a charity in your client's name. Get to know each of your clients and show genuine interest in their lives. Remember details and ask about their families and lives. Create an emotional connection any chance you are able. Once relationships have been established, attend family weddings, funerals, bar and bat mitzvahs. "Showing up" for your clients because you genuinely care about them is a sure way to solidify your connections with them.

Check in even when you have nothing to sell them. Clients love to know that you care about them beyond the sale of services. Do reach out to your clients from time to time and check in with them to see how they are doing. Take them to lunch, meet up for a game of golf; ask them about the outcome of an important family event. These ways of connecting are opportune times to find out if there is anything you could be doing even better to make this client happier than they already are.

Don't forget about your existing clients, even when your business is booming with new ones. Clients can tell when they're on the back burner. Consciously devote time to touching base with your loyal long-term clients—especially when new customers are banging down your door. Nobody wants to feel like a "third wheel," certainly not your trusted clients. Keep that connection strong and nurture it every step of the way by reaching out and staying in clear communication with your clients.

Resist going on autopilot. Even if you have your sales technique down pat, find a way to actively engage with every client. Clients can sense if you're phoning it in. Try to step into the shoes of your client each time you're having a meeting. Find ways to really connect with the human being sitting across from you and remember that you are striving to improve their lives.

Apologize if you make a mistake and fix the problem immediately. In most cases, customers aren't interested in holding grudges—they want to forgive and forget. The best way to smooth things over when you've messed up is to make a heartfelt apology and then make it right. Take a moment to address mistakes, and put in place ways to continually improve on your process by addressing obstacles that may slow down your momentum.

PART TWO

Achieving Safety

On November 6, 1962, I looked down the barrel of a fully loaded .38 caliber. It was my son's first birthday, which made it a terrible day to die. Fear is a great motivator, but not when someone is pointing a pistol at your chest.

CHAPTER SEVEN

Take a Risk

One of the first golden rules in my blueprint to success is simple: *Take a risk. It is so simple—it amazes me that most people will not take the challenge.*

Once you've achieved the ability to feed yourself and your family, Maslow will tell you that you will move on to creating personal, financial, and physical safety. After I had lost everything, I needed to figure out a way not only to support my family but to secure safety for all of us as well. The road ahead was not easy.

When you lose everything the way I did in August of 1974, you have two choices: Become a victim, paralyzed with fear, or get up and dust yourself off to rebuild your life. By now, you know which one I chose.

One of the first golden rules in my blueprint to success is simple: Take a risk. It is so simple—it amazes me that most don't take the challenge.

If you're someone who finds comfort in the stability and consistency of your paycheck, it's very risky to put yourself on the line to say, "I want to be in the top 1 percent." It's risky to have such a goal! Because when you take a risk, two things can happen: You can win or you can lose. But taking a risk can also be incredibly exciting. Just thinking of it now, I am smiling. Risking is a challenge because you're asking yourself, *Can I really do this?* It's putting yourself out there.

I am not telling you to be Nik Wallenda—who holds nine Guinness World Records for various acrobatic feats, including tight-rope walking across the Grand Canyon—but I am telling you to do something you've never done before: Go for the dream, even if it means falling down a few times and getting back up.

If we take a look at the types of professions that make up the top 1 percent of the wealth in this country, what do we have? The people on Wall Street, attorneys, real estate agents, professional athletes, entertainers, and those in the insurance industry. These are some of the professions that offer that no glass ceiling or limitation on the income level that can be earned. Look at professional athletes. There are only 626 Major League Baseball players in the U.S. That's much less than 1 percent of all of the people who are out there attempting to become professional baseball players. Yes, some real estate agents make several million dollars a year, but that represents a tiny minority. Most of them earn between two and three hundred thousand dollars a year. I know what it's like to be in the top 1 percent. I was the number one agent at Northwestern Mutual. That means that out of the 8,000 agents at the company, I was outperforming 7,999 of them. Even when I was the number two agent three different times during my career, I was still outperforming 7,998 agents. Being in the top 1 percent is a lofty goal. I am here to tell you that even though it's not easy, it's possible. In the words of the great Muhammad Ali:

> "Impossible is just a big word thrown around by small men who find it easier to live in the world they've been given than to explore the power they have to change it. Impossible is not a fact. It's an opinion. Impossible is not a declaration. It's a dare. Impossible is potential. Impossible is temporary. Impossible is nothing."

Whatever challenges you might be facing at the moment, whether you're already quite successful but would like to keep the successes rolling in, or whether you've just lost everything the way I did, I suggest you take a risk. And no, there is no safety net. If you're waiting for that safety net to cradle your possible fall, you'll never do anything; you'll never go anywhere. Create a business for yourself, build a clientele, and nurture your reputation. And guess what? You will have created a fabulous safety net.

I always say to people, "What do you have to lose?" Unless your answer is "my life," I say go for it and don't look back. Take a risk!

You Have Nothing to Lose — Unless You're Being Held at Gunpoint

For most of my career, fear has propelled me forward, motivating me to rise to the occasion. I've never been paralyzed by fear, except on the day I was held at gunpoint.

On November 6, 1962, I looked down the barrel of a fully loaded .38 caliber. It was my son's first birthday, which made it a terrible day to die. Fear is a great motivator, but not when someone is pointing a pistol at your chest.

These were the early days when I was working at Zeidler and Zeidler clothing store on Western Avenue. A man came in looking for a suit. He was built like a superhero with the waist of a teenager but the shoulders of the Hulk. He was a bull of a man who could have bench pressed little old me with just one arm.

"I don't see anything I like," he says, getting ready to walk out.

I give him my card. "If you don't find anything, come back another time." The man takes my card and walks out of the store.

I go downstairs to have lunch. While washing my hands, I hear one of the other employees call out to me, "Hey, Paul, there's a man up here to see you." When I reach the top of the stairs, I see the same *Incredible Hulk* customer standing in the middle of our store, waiting for me.

"You know what? I've changed my mind. I am going to take those two suits after all," the Hulk says. *Great!* I think. *I've just sold two Chester Lowry suits!* At $125 per suit, and with my 3 percent commission, I am feeling pretty happy. I whip off a pair of pants and roll up the cuffs.

"Come," I say, "let's go try on the pants."

We head for the fitting room. I hand the customer the pair of pants and watch him disappear as I pull the red curtains shut behind him.

"Put these on. I'll have our tailor come out."

I wait patiently on the other side of the curtain. I wait and wait and wait. Nothing. How long does it take to remove your shoes and put on a pair of pants? Eight or nine minutes go by.

"Is everything all right? Can I help you in there?"

"Yeah, I am having a little problem with these pants," he answers.

I pull the curtain open to assist him and without hesitation, the man puts a .38 caliber to my chest. I can see every single one of those brass bullets lined up 1, 2, 3, 4, 5. Each one ready to enter my heart.

"I am taking these suits. Come with me," he says.

He takes the suits, walks out of the fitting room, and puts the clothes over his arm, covering the gun, and all I can think about is, *It's my son's birthday. I don't want to die.*

We walk by the cash register. "Do you want the money?" I ask him.

"Keep walking!" he exclaims as he pushes the gun deeper into my back.

Just as we are stepping out of the store, my bosses Marvin and Lee walk in, clearly engrossed in conversation.

"Hey, Paul!"

Paralyzed by fear, I am unable to speak, and hear myself grunt in response. We walk out, leaving the owners of the store unsuspecting.

Where is this guy taking me? I wonder. I can see a J. J. Newberry store on the other side of the parking lot. Nobody uses a gun to steal two suits. He must be kidnapping me.

We walk behind J. J. Newberry. Now we are really far away from the store, too far to get anybody to help me. We arrive at a parked beige Plymouth, a beat-up junker, with dozens of crazy phrases hand-painted, saying things like "Hey mama, I'm your man" and "You're hot baby." What kind of car is this?

"Open the back door!" the Hulk says to me, pointing the gun in my direction.

"Please don't shoot me!" I hear myself yelling in a pitiful voice. "Today is my son's first birthday!"

"Open the damn door!"

I open the back door of the car.

"Throw the suits in!"

I do as he orders.

"Don't move. If you move, I'll kill you!"

Standing there in broad daylight at the back of the J. J. Newberry store, I watch the car drive away.

I am not a sprint runner but that day I ran faster than I have ever run in my entire life. I ran down the 14 stairs leading to the basement office of the store and stormed in where my boss was on the phone.

"I have to call the police," I yelled trying to push him out of the way. But I was too nervous and too shaken to be able to dial and let Lee call for me instead.

Two hours later, they caught the Hulk at a tailor shop on Western Avenue. He was getting the two suits altered. The car he was driving was so distinctive that he might as well have been driving the only orange and purple Rolls-Royce in town with a big sign on it that read *Here I am!* Later, when I testified in court, I found out he had been in prison for beating an old man nearly to death. It was 1962, my son had just turned one, and I had just escaped a gun being pointed at my heart. I was a very lucky 23-year-old.

Rising from the Ashes: Starting a New Life

So unless you're being held at gunpoint, you should be risking everything for a chance to move your life to higher ground. Years after that terrifying incident when I was held at gunpoint, I did risk everything in order to start a new life after bankruptcy. How did I do it? I took the ultimate risk by making a 180-degree career change and jumped into an industry I knew nothing about. I put everything on the line and went for it.

Here I was at 36 in the throes of bankruptcy. My friend Hershey, who was my insurance agent, said to me, "I want you to go into the insurance business."

I said to him, "Are you kidding me? Hershey, do I look like an insurance man? This is not my image." In my ignorance, I mistakenly thought there was nothing glamorous about the insurance business.

"What image are you talking about?"

"I don't know. I just don't think of myself as an insurance man."

"What is it that you think of me then?"

"Are you kidding me?" I said. "I love you. I think you're just the best."

"Well, people might not like the insurance industry but they are very fond of the person who handles their insurance," Hershey told me. And he was right. We are all so busy making judgments in our lives, left and right. What did I know about the insurance business? Nothing, except what Hershey had related to me. I knew I needed to work. Even though my attorney had found a job for me at Sally Shops, a women's retail chain, I also began the interviewing process to become an insurance agent. Not knowing what direction to take, I took both jobs. I signed a contract with Northwestern Mutual even though I was employed at Sally Shops. I did not know what direction I was going to take. I am not proud to admit this but for the first three months of my work at Northwestern Mutual, where I would end up working for the next 42 incredible years, I also worked at Sally Shops where I got free tires for the car Joyce had managed to keep from being repossessed. I was torn and conflicted about my choice, but I desperately needed income. Sally Shops was my comfort zone; it was familiar and reminded me of everything I already knew, having owned my own stores. But something deep was pushing me to go beyond what I knew and pursue a new opportunity. I took the ultimate risk: a brand-new business I knew nothing about and went from the frying pan to the fire. I left my comfort zone for a chance at a new horizon.

I took to the insurance business like a duck to water. My first day in the business, I said to myself: *Wow, I love this.* I knew immediately I had found my home. I had been so fearful up until that point. But the minute I committed, I thought: *This is wonderful. I am changing people's lives by providing them with great security. This is a meaningful endeavor. I am thrilled that I took the risk.*

How did I get started? Simple. I used the important rule of a successful business: contacting people in your existing network.

I took a yellow legal pad and I wrote down the 125 names in my Rolodex from the clothing business. I called every single one of those 125 names. Three became clients who in turn yielded 27 referred leads! Creating referred leads is the key to success for any business. I don't care if you're selling insurance, real estate, cars, or mattresses. As a professional, you need to have new clients referred to you. You want to establish a relationship with people in a business or simply a client and you want that person to be happy and satisfied with the service and product you're providing. You want them to think of your service as being superior so they can refer you to other people. The process of keeping your business alive and getting the client to give you referrals is the crux of any profession.

Maybe you're in real estate and you have sold the Smith family their first home. They love the house; they're happy. Now you want them to go tell all of their friends who might be in the market for a new home how happy they are with your services. You want each and every single one of your clients to give you referred leads. This is an ongoing process that never stops. Because every time you make a sale, you're out of inventory. You need a continuum. The only time you can get that continuum is for your clients to feel that you're providing a valuable service for them.

So that day when I picked up my list of 125 names and sold three contracts, they in turn went on to provide me with another ten more clients over the next few years. When you sell something to a client, always ask them, "Do you know anyone else who might be interested in my services?" Always ask your clients for referred leads.

In June of 1977, I hired my assistant, Toba Weinstock. She worked with me for 38 years. Over the years, she made sure I had a lot of appointments. I worked hard. I was always on the phone to get more appointments. And even though in the beginning I started from scratch, I built up my business to reach 5,000 policies on the books with a large staff and a very large payroll. It took a lot of work and I loved every minute of it.

Looking back, my bankruptcy was a blessing. There were times during my career in the insurance business when I made more money in three weeks, sometimes even in one week, than I had made in an entire year working in the clothing business.

Over the years, I have asked myself if I could have avoided bankruptcy. The fact is that in life there is good luck, bad luck, and no luck. Throughout my life, I've had a bit of each. What could I have done to stop my bankruptcy, even if I caught my thieving employee? What if he never stole anything? I still would have gone bankrupt. Because of the economy. Because I had no business sense. Because I was not minding the store. Because I thought that I was the king of the hill, when in fact I was not. And because I needed to learn the lessons from these experiences. Timing is everything. What if I would have gone in the insurance business earlier? Maybe I would have made more money, or maybe I would not have been as successful. Who knows? *What if* that light had turned red rather than green, and so on and so on? These things are impossible to predict. Some things are out of our control. It is pointless to ask "what if" questions. Timing is everything.

One thing is for sure: One of the biggest victories of my life was to be able to come out of my bankruptcy with dignity and respect. That was my first victory in a series of many victories. But in order for me to keep the victories coming, I would have to master many new skills of business. The first of these skills is simple enough: Look, speak, and act the part. Are you willing and able to take the risk to change your life?

Life Lesson Moment

The challenge of this chapter, dear reader, is to let go of your fear. If you're struggling to pay your bills, know that I have been in your shoes. I have stayed up many nights wondering how I would be able to make ends meet. So if you're sitting here reading my book and saying to yourself, *This is all well and good but I need to make the mortgage next month*, then I am here to remind you that you're approaching this puzzle from the wrong angle. Remember, as a kid, the story of the cookie jar? Don't get caught with your hand in the cookie jar.

Close your eyes. Can you think of a time when you let go of a limited mindset in your life and gained a whole new reality as a result? If you answered "no," don't worry; it is never too late to begin taking incremental steps in your life in order to make changes that bring you closer to who you really are. The more you take these leaps in the direction of the *real* you, the more you will begin to trust yourself. After all, the most important relationship you will ever have in your life is with yourself. Trust that taking the first step towards becoming the person you truly are is exactly where you need to be today.

Now, write down the worst-case scenarios in one column as a result of going for your dream career, and in the second column write down what you can gain from building that fruitful career. Which column wins? I can already tell you without a doubt that the column of the dream career wins every time. I know this because I have lived it. Remember that job I took because it offered new tires for my car? I let it go and took a leap of faith. When I look back today, I can tell you that the security of that job pales in comparison to the life I built going for my dream career in the insurance business. Once you let go of that fear, you will make room for the changes you can make today. There is no greater feeling than being who you really are.

How to Build a Referral System That Gets Results

Regardless of the type of business you're in, referrals are the key to success. When clients feel cared for, referrals follow. My average client would purchase seven contracts from me and in turn would refer me to the folks they respect and like, either through their personal and social networks or their business contacts. I also gained a great number of referrals by way of the countless charities to which I donated not only my money but my time. Referrals will keep your business flourishing.

Action Steps

Identify untapped clients in your network. Take a moment to identify contacts in your business, social, or family networks who may be potential clients themselves or know of new potential clients. Chances are, there are many contacts in your network who could be contacted and converted into clients.

Attend every single industry event you can. Make a list on a quarterly basis of industry events you could attend in order to keep up with competing businesses, stay on top of trends, and become aware of new client markets.

Schedule meetings with former clients to get referrals. When do you ask for referrals? At the end of a transaction, after the client has had the opportunity to see the work you have done and you've established a solid relationship of trust. Who are your former clients? Schedule a meeting with them now.

Take full advantage of online networking sites like LinkedIn. Keep your profile active and up-to-date. Make sure your business also has an active and well-curated Facebook, Instagram, or Twitter account with interesting thought leader-style blogs, podcasts, and articles.

Connect with other professionals outside of your industry. High-powered professionals need and want to hire other high-powered professionals such as doctors, lawyers, venture capitalists, and CEOs of various companies. Take a look at ways you can connect with these professionals outside of your industry and reach out to them.

Create your own face-to-face networking events for your online contacts. Establish relationships with organizations and businesses and organize events where you can offer your expertise. You can capture your social media networks, along with all of your other potential connections, by holding a mixer or open house, or offering a free presentation where you can talk one-on-one with many perspective clients. Make sure to include Facebook friends, people you've never met, and friends of clients in your invitation.

Help charities and non-profits. Donate your time and money to charities, share your expertise on boards of directors, attend galas, mixers, and other charity social events. Your involvement with charity work will enrich your professional and personal relationships and indirectly expand your reach of potential clients.

Cultivate your personal life to expand your referral pool. If you only stay in your office working, it limits your exposure to new clients. But getting active and involved in your local community opens you up to meeting others who might be looking for your services. So join a local religious organization, a common interest group, a gym, a country club, an amateur sports league, and build your network while having fun and enjoying your life.

CHAPTER EIGHT

Look, Speak, and Act the Part

When you walk into the Northwestern Mutual *building in Milwaukee, you will see that it is gleaming. It's a very old and distinguished piece of architecture—like one of those old European buildings. But every piece of brass sparkles. There are people whose entire job is to polish the brass. The stairway is marble. Walking in, you know you're in a substantial company and feel secure.*

Look the Part

As I got ready to go to work, I stood in front of the mirror and said to myself, *Would you buy insurance from somebody who looks like this?* I always made sure my answer was a resounding "yes."

If you're going to be in the business world, then you need to look, speak, and act like a businessperson. You could be the most Pulitzer Prize-winning, MBA-having genius in your field, but if you don't look the part, you will have to work harder than necessary to gain credibility. When you walk into the headquarters of the Northwestern Mutual columned building at 720 E. Wisconsin Avenue in Milwaukee, you see a beautiful, imposing eight-story neoclassical building with sophisticated Corinthian columns and a marble stair-case. As you walk into the lobby, you feel secure. This structure built in 1914 expresses *reliability*. The lobby is gleaming—every piece of brass sparkles. The company has hired people whose entire job is to polish the brass of the railings. Why does an insurance company have such a building for its headquarters? Simple answer: It inspires confidence and security. Image is everything.

You Want to Win? Dress Like a Winner

The other day, a friend of the family wanted to pick my brain about business, so he took me out to lunch. When he greeted me, I couldn't believe my eyes: His shoes were scuffed; his shirt was wrin-kled. His appearance was generally unkempt. How was this man go-ing to succeed in business with such an appearance?

I've always lived by the credo that a polished and professional image is crucial in establishing successful relationships. After all, the first thing a person sees when you walk into their office is you! You never get a second chance to make a first impression.

Speaking of attire, I had a neighbor many years ago whose father owned the company Gulfstream Jets. In 1985, Chrysler bought Gulf-stream for $637 million. Part of their strategy was to diversify into a high-tech industry. It was also that year that Gulfstream appeared on the Fortune 500 list at #417. These G3 and G5 airplanes are mighty powerful machines. The wealthiest of the wealthy buy those planes. My neighbor worked out of his home office selling these jets for his father's company.

Each morning, he would wake, have breakfast, take a shower and get dressed in the most elegant and professional attire. Then, he would walk two doors down from his bedroom to his home office and go to work. You might wonder, why wear a suit and tie if no one is going to see him? The answer is simple: He looked the part and it gave him confidence. Looking the part made him feel profes-sional. This man was working and when he got on the phone with multi-millionaire clients, he wanted to feel and look sharp. I love that story because it illustrates my view on the importance of image in the quest for success.

One day my office manager Toba asked if we could have Casual Fridays. My response was, "We are professionals, we are in business, and we are dealing with clients. We must look like professionals. So, I am now giving you permission to have casual Saturday—on your day off." Psychologically speaking, it is crucial to dress the part because it helps you operate more professionally and approach your work with more self-confidence.

Image is not only important in business, but in every aspect of life. My wife, Joyce, and I love music. We love to go to the opera and to the symphony. We have noticed that people today don't dress appropriately when attending special events. This bothers me. Why dress like you're going to the County Fair, if you're going to the opera? When you don't bother to dress accordingly, it is disrespectful not only to the performers but also to yourself.

When I go see clients, I am always impeccable. Everything about my appearance is flawless. My Montblanc briefcase paints the image of success. I look like somebody who really knows what they're doing. Looking the part is a crucial aspect of conducting a successful business. When you look the part, you can sit back and watch as doors open, offering you access to the people and the resources that you need in order to be successful. Your image is of the utmost importance.

Speak the Part: People Respond with Conviction

Here's an interesting phenomenon: If you look the part and speak with conviction, people are more inclined to trust you and perceive you as a leader. This level of self-confidence in turn enhances your credibility and allows you to inhabit a space with ease.

The power of conviction cannot be better illustrated than in the powerful movie *Bridge of Spies*. Every American should see this movie. During the height of the Cold War, a man named Francis Gary Powers flew a U-2 spy plane taking aerial photographs of the Soviet Union. Perceiving him as a threat, the Soviets shot his plane down. Powers was captured and sentenced to ten years in prison. His only hope was the New York insurance lawyer named Donovan (played by Tom Hanks) who was delegated to negotiate his release. The plan was for Donovan to trade a convicted Soviet spy in exchange for Powers. Tom Hanks' character was so tenacious and so convincing that he managed to get the Russians to not only release Powers but another prisoner as well. The power of conviction can have tremendous beneficial effects on the outcome of a situation.

Here's an interesting story about the power of conviction. As part of my continuing education and growth in my career, I would go and listen to talks given by experts in my field. So one day, I went to Pasadena to hear a gentleman talk about a product called "non-qualified deferred compensation," where a portion of the employee's salary was deferred until a specified date.

I like this product. So, I say to myself, *This is for me. I want to sell it.*

The *Los Angeles Times* publishes a list of the top 100 companies in the county. I get a copy of it, and each week, I send out a letter to ten businesses on the list, in order to introduce myself and my product. Following up on my letter, I start making calls to these companies on my list and sure enough one of them is interested. Wow! But what do I know about non-qualified deferred compensation? My knowledge is limited. The potential client says to me, "We would like to talk to a company that already has one of these plans in place to get their input."

So I say, "Great! I will get back to you with that information." Being that I had no experience in selling a non-qualified deferred compensation policy—because I never sold one—I had to get more knowledge on the product.

Unfortunately, I didn't have anybody in mind for them to contact and get that kind of information. I call an associate in San Francisco, the same expert whose talk I'd heard in Pasadena. I say, "I have this prospective client but they want to talk to a chief financial officer of a company that already has this plan in place. Could you refer me to one of your clients and see if they will talk to my prospect and give their input?"

He says, "Paul, I have to tell you something."

"What?" I ask.

"I've never sold one of these plans."

Now you might wonder how someone who has never sold a non-qualified deferred compensation plan can consider themselves an expert on the topic. Wait, it gets better. So, I hang up the phone and continue on my search for someone who might be able to talk to this potential client. One of our agents puts me in touch with a man who had just retired from Northwestern Mutual and gave speeches all over the United States on this topic. I call him.

"Hi, I am working with this company in Southern California and they want to talk to someone who already has a non-qualified deferred compensation plan," I tell the man on the other line.

"Well, Paul, I have to tell you the truth. I've never sold one," he tells me.

Are you starting to see a pattern here? Now I am beginning to realize something crucial: When you speak with conviction, people will declare that you're an expert in your field, even if you've never put your knowledge into action. Here were these two men speaking with absolute conviction about a topic for which they had very little firsthand knowledge. And yet they had hundreds of people listening to them. They had great credentials and great credibility. It was so strange that it was actually funny. I thought to myself: *Oh my goodness, what do I do now?*

This experience says that if you speak with conviction, and with great knowledge, you gain credibility.

Following this incident, I sold a number of non-qualified deferred compensation plans, all coming to fruition today. And people who are collecting their money love it and are calling me to tell me that

I am their hero. I became *the expert* because I spoke with the power of conviction and most importantly because I garnered extensive knowledge about deferred compensation.

Whenever you are trailblazing through unknown territory and attempting to do something new, *move forward, take the risk, do it.* What do you have to lose?

Act the Part

If you wish to be a professional, you have two choices: Go out and get a job with career potential or go into business for yourself. I chose the latter. It takes a special kind of person to be an entrepreneur. Thriving businesses require a lot of hard work and the motivation to stay abreast of all of the various tasks and responsibilities. Most of life is mundane, and the thrill of landing a deal lasts a few short minutes, but getting there and repeating it, then pulling it off again and again, require long-term foresight. Success requires the sustained effort of staying on top of daily tasks by avoiding short cuts, building trust, and remaining engaged with clients. In other words, being a professional requires that you not only *look* the part but also *act* it as well.

One of the greatest qualities I have cultivated in myself during the course of my career is my tenacity and my ability to not lose track of my goals. This quality has served me well over the years. Some of my initial contacts did not become clients until several years after our initial meeting, yet this did not stop me from maintaining a relationship with them and remaining available in the event they would become interested in my services. This was the case for a group of three doctors I had contacted at Good Samaritan Hospital as a result of a referral. After my first visit with them, they said to me, "Thanks for coming out, but we're fine." I have a system in place that allows me to contact my prospective clients twice a year. Every six months for five years, I contacted those three doctors/prospective clients before they decided to take me up on my services and become clients. Tenacity can take you from a floundering business to a flourishing one.

When you land the client of your dreams or you launch that desired career, it is very important that you maintain the momentum. Some of the things that you can do in order to move forward in your career is to develop your skills, attend conferences, and continue to work your craft. This is what I strived to do. I continuously read all of the journals in my field and attended continuing education seminars. The fact is, the learning process never stops; it goes on forever.

The Importance of Making Appointments

For 40 years, I never strayed from giving my business steady and consistent effort to make appointments with potential clients. In every business, new clients are your life-blood. Regardless of the industry you're in, you will need to establish contact with the people you're serving by establishing a solid foundation of trust and providing the finest service at the center of each relationship. In any business, you must establish a reliable method of obtaining clients: making ten phone calls that would yield three appointments, which would in turn result in obtaining a new client.

I cannot stress enough the importance of setting up appointments for the week. In your own business, this may look slightly different, but the bottom line is the same: You're not focusing on dollars, but you do have to take the right steps to procure new clients. This process should never stop. In fact, your business is at your most vulnerable when you become complacent and believe that you have enough clients. You can never have too many clients. Well, I should not say *never* because you could in fact reach a point when your existing infrastructure is no longer sufficient to deal with the number of clients coming through your door. And then you must increase your staff to accommodate your growth. But ultimately you must obtain new clients on a regular basis.

The first thing that comes to light when you look at this formula is the fact that you have to make a lot of phone calls before you can acquire a client. I have found that you have to talk to ten people before one of them becomes one of your clients. Phone calls were never my favorite activity. But I would build them into my weekly schedule and block out time on two different afternoons when I did nothing but make phone calls. And whenever I noticed that things were slower than I liked, I would build in additional time and say to myself: *Tomorrow, I am going to make as many phone calls as I need because my goal for the day is not three appointments, but four.* So what do I have to do to make that happen? I have to work an extra hour and make additional calls. I have to close my door to my office and not listen to the outside prattle.

Handling the Phone Call

When I call, I say, "Hello, this is Paul Krasnow from Northwestern Mutual. Do you have a moment to talk?"

And you'll probably say "no."

"When is a good time to talk?" I'll ask you.

"What is this about?" you'll most likely answer, as you try to get off the phone.

"Your good friend and my client, 'So-and-So,' has a service with me and felt that it is important for me to share some information with you about my services."

Now that I have mentioned the person who has made the referral, I have your attention. Without the referral, I could have never made the call.

"How about Tuesday or Thursday?"

Notice that you haven't heard me say what I do. All you heard me say was that "So-and-So" has a service that he loves and that he wants me to share it with you. The key is to get you to agree to see me. Once I have you in person, I have increased my chances greatly for you to become one of my clients.

All I want is an appointment.

All I want is a client.

And I am not focused on commission.

Making the Initial Appointment

It's difficult to get that initial appointment. You might be the best in your business and the best in your field, but the prospect does not know you. That's the tough part. In my business, the nature of the appointment is not the easiest to bring up. *Geez, I don't really want to talk to my insurance person about my death or how I might become severely disabled after a massive stroke.* Not an easy conversation to have. The key is to get them face-to-face. Once that happens, I've reduced my numbers from ten to three to one. In other words, for every three potential clients I meet face-to-face, one becomes an actual client. These are much better odds than my initial ten-to-one phone to client ratio.

When I make an appointment, I say to my prospective client, "Would you like your spouse to be here? Would you like her involved in this process?" He may or may not want to involve his wife, but the mere fact that I have invited her to be there sets the tone—I care about my clients. When they go home, they will talk to their spouses and say, "Honey, I talked with Paul Krasnow and he invited you to the meeting. Would you like to come?"

"Paul invited me to the meeting?" the spouse will ask, intrigued. I have established a differential.

Keep Your Word — Build Trust

So we schedule a 15-minute appointment and I don't go over that duration no matter what. I can cover most of what I need to say in just five minutes and then I leave the remaining ten minutes for questions. Let's assume this potential client has an interest and they want to continue the conversation. I never extend the meeting. Not even by a minute. You might be wondering, *Why not extend the meeting if I have the time, and this person seems really interested?* But I assure you it's not a good idea. Here's why.

When approaching potential clients, the key is to have a clear plan and stick to it. In part this is good practice because it allows the client to not feel overwhelmed with the nature of our talk, but also it builds implicit trust with them. If I say to you that we are going to talk for 15 minutes, we are going to talk for 15 minutes. My word is worth a pound of gold.

Every interaction you have with a client determines whether or not they will trust you. In my case, my clients can trust me, right off the bat.

Once we sit down to talk, I get to the point. I stick to the plan and I make eye contact. The only things I write down are the key points of personal information like their date of birth, the name of their wife and children, and other basic elements of that nature. A typical opening to my meeting with my prospective client might go something like this:

"Your friend and my client 'So-and-So' felt that it was extremely important that you see me. There has been a revolution in the insurance industry, and he felt that you would benefit from hearing about it."

It is important to mention the referral that links you to this potential client. I do all of my client contacts by referral because there is an implicit bond between the friend and the prospect.

Sticking to the appointment duration of fifteen minutes tells the client the following:

1. I respect you.
2. I am going to do everything I can to earn your trust.
3. I don't want to waste your time.

You have just accomplished the hardest part of the process: getting a potential client to meet with you face-to-face. Once you're in front of the prospect, there is a good chance business will be born out of the meeting. Remember the formula:

Ten calls,

Three appointments,

One client.

Ten-three-one.

Truly Listen

Once you have succeeded in making phone calls and setting up appointments with your prospects, you must master the primordial skill of actively listening to the potential client during the meeting. Most people don't listen to each other. Instead, they get caught up in the hustle and bustle of their lives and they move so fast they are missing what is going on around them. My experiences in the insurance business have given me an opportunity to learn and discipline myself to really listen to people. You will find that most people are starved to be heard and want the opportunity to talk. The minute people find someone who really listens to them, they open up and begin to speak frankly from the heart.

Many people come home from work and find their spouse taking care of the children or working on a project and are too busy to talk. Sure, they use words, but they don't actually hear one another. There is no communication. What a great gift it is to have somebody really listen to you. What a wonderful thing!

Listening to my clients over the years has been one of the fundamental tools I have used to build trust with them and establish a rock-solid relationship. Throughout my career, I have learned to apply active listening skills and to REALLY take in what my clients are saying. Some people start talking and immediately stop listening. What was supposed to be a conversation is actually a monologue. They are already crafting a response to what the other person is saying while that person is still talking. They are not fully listening. You'd be amazed how powerful it can be to listen to another person, to really listen and gain a sense of their perspective. Without active listening skills, you can never build a relationship of trust and a solid foundation with others.

If you're a lawyer, an accountant, a real estate person, or a doctor, etc., then the above applies a thousand-fold. How can you sell a house without knowing what the person really wants? As a lawyer, how can you represent someone without knowing about their problems or aspirations? If you're in the people business, nothing matters more than listening.

My career speaks for itself. I am a living example of a great listener. You do not write 5,000 contracts and $2 billion worth of business if you're not listening and absorbing and being empathetic and understanding of your clients' needs, wants, and dreams.

I realized the benefits of my listening skills when one day one of my early clients who had been recording our meetings for 20 years said to me, "Everything I told you that I wanted has come to fruition." This client had recently listened to all of our recorded conversations of the past 20 years and was amazed that the financial goals we had set together had come true. I was happy for him but I was not surprised. Time and time again, I have seen the power of my listening skills and my ability to work with my clients to nurture their goals. That, dear reader, is the power of active listening and nurtured client relationships.

Engage with Your Clients—Be Dynamic

If listening is key, remaining engaged during your interaction with your clients is also equally important. This is true of any industry or job you might be in. If you're a professor at a university, for example, you're either in great demand or you're disliked by your students. Why is that? The answer is simple. The professors who engage with their students by being dynamic and acknowledging their needs come across as fascinating and interesting. These are the professors students seek out. The educators who just bore their students because they'd rather hear themselves speak instead of actually connecting with their students, these are the people whose work is simply not in great demand. Which one would you rather be?

The same is true in business. You don't have to talk to your clients every day but you do have to stay connected so that they are reminded of you and of your services. It is important both your current and potential clients know that you remember and care about them.

If you're in the health industry, a cardiologist for example, you can share helpful information about the latest advancements in cardiology with patients. It's the same if you're a lawyer or an accountant. It is important to keep your clients up to date on what's going on in their particular industry. Stay connected and relevant.

The bottom line is this: Are you expressing genuine concern for your clients or are you simply going through the motions mindlessly without engaging with them on an authentic level? People always know when you genuinely have their best interest at heart.

After the First Appointment

Now that you have mastered listening and remaining engaged, you are ready to meet with your clients. What should your next plan of action be?

A typical day for me was being out all day with appointments and then going back into the office and having my assistant, Toba, send out discovery letters to those clients with whom I had met for the first time. The letter would go something like this:

"Dear prospective client: Here is a recap of what we discussed in our meeting today…"

And I would go over what we talked about. If we set up a follow-up meeting, then I would add:

"I will see you next Tuesday at 2:00."

Toba worked long hours and never left the office before 7:00 at night. She would send out the discovery letter. Then on the business day prior to the next appointment, Toba would call just to confirm the upcoming meeting. Once that was taken care of, I would do a fact finder about the client's assets, income, goals, etc., and organize all of the elements needed for them to paint a clear picture of their future. This would allow me to build a financial program for them. Then Toba would send another letter just to go over the salient points of our meeting and to outline everything we would be doing in the upcoming appointment. It is also in that letter that I would discuss money.

Let's say that during our initial meeting, you conveyed to me that you could allocate $2,240 a month for you and your wife in order to provide for your security in the event of an early death or living too long. You have also told me that you need $5 million of coverage for your family when you die. Your needs are specific. Now I go out on our next appointment and provide you with solutions to provide you with that security you are seeking. And with your permission, before we meet, I have talked to your attorney and your accountant in order to introduce myself and let them know what I am doing with you.

Regardless of your profession, it is crucial that you remain engaged and in touch with your potential clients after the initial contact. The exact method of communication may vary and should suit your particular needs; it may come in the form of a letter, as was the case for me. Or you may decide to call your contact instead. Regardless of the ways you decide to customize this approach for your own purpose, make sure you keep the momentum of your initial contact with this potential client alive.

The Follow-up Meeting

If the initial meeting went well with you as my potential client and you're interested in going to the next level, then we would schedule that second appointment and explore your financial dreams, desires, and needs. At this point in our relationship, it is important that you know you're meeting with a professional and that you're in good hands.

Even though your financial situation might be good today, I am here to simplify your life and help you find a way to secure your future today. Here's what I'd say to you:

"You're making a comfortable living, but you're living above your means and you are not saving for your future." This is the point where I would build a plan with you in order to craft a solid and stable financial future for yourself and your family in incremental stages. We would identify key steps you can take today and agree to reassess each year in order to determine where you are in reaching your financial goals.

As you sit here with me securing your future, it is easy to realize how fast the last ten years of your life have gone. Don't you think it all went by in a flash? If I snap my fingers, can you see that you'll be 60, just like that? My question to you, dear reader, and to any of my potential clients is simple: When do you want to start securing your life and creating something that is meaningful to you?

Even though you may not have the necessary resources today to do everything you want to do, we're going to start with small steps in our overall financial plan in order to allow you to get closer to your goals each year.

As my client, I never shock you by suggesting you put away more money than is financially feasible. When doing financial planning, you must be realistic when you suggest a plan to meet the client's needs. Instead, we incrementally move through achievable steps that improve your life more and more each year, bringing you closer to your goals and the life you want.

Regardless of the nature of your business or whether your goal is to be the CEO of a company or the owner of your small business, looking and acting the part and mastering these few basic business skills will take you across the threshold to a successful career.

Life Lesson Moment

Take a moment to examine your current situation. Can you honestly say that you are looking and acting the part as you build your dream career? If your answer is "yes," do you think there are ways that you can improve and strengthen your image in order to draw the desired clients your way? Whether your answer to this question was "yes" or "no," take a moment to make a list of the ways you can improve your image today. Remember that everything you do and say must exude an aura of confidence. It is crucial that you reflect back to your client the core values and essence of what you are offering them in your services. For example, if you're in the health and wellness profession, it is crucial that your image and lifestyle reflect the values associated with this line of business. Are there ways that you can instill those qualities you are offering your clients in your own life? Sometimes, improving your image can mean making small changes, like buying a new suit or changing your haircut.

If these suggestions seem trivial, think about the power-posing experiment carried out by Amy Cuddy, a social psychologist at the Harvard Business School. She researched the effects of taking on certain power poses before important events in order to boost confidence. Taking on a power pose is the conscious decision to make your body big by doing things like opening your arms, elevating them above your head, spreading your legs as you stand. Not only did Cuddy evaluate the impact taking on power poses can have on the level of the subject's performance in events like a job interview, but she also measured the impact it had on physiological changes taking place in the body. Cuddy discovered that people who take on high-power poses such as standing tall, opening their chest up, and raising their arms up in the air for two minutes prior to a business encounter resulted in higher and more successful performances. Not only did they feel and act more confidently, but on a physiological level, their bodies demonstrated 25 percent lower levels of cortisol and an 8 percent increase in the dominance hormone testosterone. Looking and acting the part has a genuine impact on the level of success you can and will achieve in your career. Cuddy will tell you that making small tweaks in your appearance and performance can result in big changes. I highly recommend watching Amy Cuddy's TED talk on the subject.

How to Build the Image of a Winner

Looking the part is an important aspect of building a successful career. When your appearance reflects the quality of your services, you will instill trust in your clients and potential clients alike. Think of your health and the wellness of your physical self as an investment towards your success. A healthy mind and body and spirit are the foundation of a healthy business.

Action Steps

Treat your body like a temple. Without the vitality and strength of your body, it is difficult to have the stamina to build a successful business. Make sure that you get plenty of sleep (seven to nine hours a night); eat a well-balanced, low-fat, high-vegetable diet; and exercise at least three to four times a week. Maintain this regimen for the rest of your life and you will be able to enjoy the fruits of your labor in your silver years.

Get rid of your destructive habits. Having destructive habits simply slows you down and makes you dependent on substances, which in turn weakens your ability to be effective and productive. Take care of healing your dependence on smoking, junk food, and any addictive substances. Don't be afraid to ask for help if you feel you are battling an addiction. You are not alone.

Really think about your image. Sadly, a mismatched image can derail a talented person's trajectory. Make sure that both your projected and actual image are actually aligned. A 25-year-old actor should have a different energy and aesthetic than a 42-year-old executive. Project power and communicate your success by way of your well-developed image.

Curate a killer wardrobe. Your clothing should communicate the exact message you want to send. You don't have to spend a fortune, but make sure everything you buy fits well and aligns with the image you want to create. If you need help, use a personal shopper and make sure your clothes fit you properly. Develop a sense of fashion. If you need a closet overhaul, start with a few well-made versatile basics, and build your wardrobe from there. Get rid of worn items or clothing that does not fit well anymore.

Accessorize appropriately. Pay attention to the details, because they also contribute to your overall image. Eyewear, jewelry, briefcases, purses, phones, fountain pens, and even your car (along with its cleanliness) should convey the exact message you intend. Everything matters.

Go the extra mile to look good. This isn't about vanity. People really are judged by their appearances. When you first meet a prospective client, the first thing they see is you. So take extra measures to keep your skin, hair, and nails in peak condition. Care for your nails, make sure your shoes are shined, and get regular age-appropriate haircuts.

Watch your posture and mannerisms. Studies have been conducted on the effects of good or poor posture on the quality of business interactions. Having good posture sends signals to your brain that you are in charge and are a winner, which in turn affects the way people perceive you. Do not underestimate the power of posture in the outcome of a business meeting.

Mind your manners. If you're sharing meals with business partners, be particularly mindful of your table manners. Avoid the use of profanity or "off color" jokes that may offend. Redirect the conversation whenever topics of politics or religion come up, even if you seem to be in agreement.

CHAPTER NINE

Do What You Need to Do So You Can Do What You Want to Do

You can't take potential to the bank. What matters in the end is what you do end up doing with your life, not what you could have or should have done.

When I look at my life today, I relish the fact that I have reaped the benefits of the success I created for myself. When I traveled first class across the world to hold an orangutan in Borneo or ate the most delectable meal at a Michelin three-star restaurant in Paris, I realized that I had managed to carry out the tasks that I needed to do in order to do what I wanted to do. This is a simple rule but it will really allow you to live and enjoy the life you've always wanted for yourself.

Showing Up Is NOT Half the Battle

I really dislike that cliché statement "showing up is half the bat-tle." Where did this fallacy come from? No entrepreneur who has built their business up from scratch will ever agree with that state-ment simply because it isn't true. Showing up is important, yes, but it is certainly NOT half the battle. I would say it's probably only one-quarter of the battle. Do you know why? Because even if you're quite good at doing something, you will have to continuously edu-cate yourself along the way. Life is a perpetual learning experience. You have to remain on top of your skills in your business but also remain relevant to what is happening within your industry. In other words, you have to know what you're doing at all times. Preparedness is most important. You can't flounder. You have to be a professional. Once you've educated yourself to become the expert in your field, you have to work hard, smart, and diligently for the entirety of your career in order to stay ahead of the curve.

When I go into a meeting, I am prepared. When I was number one in sales at Northwestern Mutual, I sold hundreds of millions of dollars of insurance to very large and renowned companies. This did not happen without preparedness, nor did it happen overnight. There are moments when we are called to bring in every skill and every piece of knowledge we have ever acquired to the challenge of a lifetime. This was the case when my company, Northwestern Mutu-al, became one of four companies to vie to provide a potential client with a deferred compensation plan.

So here we were, four opposing agents from four different compa-nies. One of the competitors was an especially formidable opponent, and I had no idea if I would close this case or not.

The meeting took place in Olympia, Washington, in a gorgeous building with a conference room overlooking Mount Rainier.

I was the last of four to give a presentation. Just before my turn came, the executive board went on a break, emptying the room. This gave me the opportunity to go into the conference room and make some opportune changes. You see, the room was set up so that my back was facing Mount Rainier, giving participants full view of this majestic mountain. Because of this distraction, I realized that nobody was going to pay much attention to what I was about to say. Instead, they would be looking outside at the beautiful view. I decided to reconfigure the setup so that the presentation board was placed in a way that ensured the participants were now focused on me. I was now looking at the majestic view and the participants were now looking at me. I knew this would give me a better chance to succeed.

So the executives walked into the room and noticed the change.

"Oh, what happened to the room?" the president of the company asked.

"There was too much of a glare, so I moved a few things around. I hope you don't mind," I answered.

Part of the story of success is being proactive. This is also an example of taking leadership.

The other three agents presenting that day had PowerPoint presentations. I never use PowerPoint. Why? Because I don't like how the room gets a little dark, making it difficult to see the reaction coming from the participants. Instead, I use the display board where I draw and write my power phrases. I keep my presentation simple and assume the prospective clients have no knowledge of the topic at hand. Ninety seconds into my presentation, as I drew my graphs on the board, the president suddenly slammed his hand down on the table, "Now I've got it. I understand this completely!" Sometimes the simplicity of a symbol or word on a board speaks best to an audience. Just like that, I had personalized my presentation and made a connection with my listeners. I had taken charge of the room and focused them on what was important. Deciding to change the configuration of the room was an altering decision that reminded me that I was able to think on my feet and harness my creative skills in order to succeed.

This anecdote may convince you that showing up is not half the battle. Showing up and being prepared is the whole battle.

As you become more and more comfortable in your business, you may find it easier to take control of your meetings. I cannot stress enough how experience and learning from your past mistakes is the key to becoming an efficient businessperson. Each day on the job is a learning experience that never stops. The errors you will inevitably make can teach you a world of knowledge on how to move forward more efficiently and hone your skills. Showing up, as I said earlier, is not half the battle. Showing up with knowledge and experience ensures a successful career.

Develop Your Personal Code of Ethics

Remember the exercise I asked you to do in Chapter 6 on identifying your core values? Now is the time for you to go one step further and develop your own personal code of ethics. What is a *personal code of ethics?* It is your own sense of what is *right* and what is *wrong,* within the bounds of legal actions. I am not so much talking about whether or not you will be tempted to break the law because, for the sake of this argument, we will assume that you will not. But I am going one step further here and urging you to develop a clear sense of the code of ethics you will apply at the core of your business.

In order to develop your own personal code of ethics, you must ask yourself questions such as, *Is this the type of client we would like to serve? What impact does this service have on our community? Do I believe in the ethical impact of my product?*

In other words, your personal code of ethics will represent the rudder that will allow you to decide the direction in which you will take your business as you make decisions along the way.

Doing What Feels Right

I have come across people along the way who did not have their clients' best interest at heart. As a professional, you have the choice to provide the best service and the best product without considering your compensation. If you follow this credo of ethics of putting your clients' best interest first, you will never have a knot in your throat when the phone rings and think, *Oh my God, who is that on the other end of the phone? Did they catch me?* Instead, you will simply build a great reputation while your business grows exponentially.

During the course of my career, I have had folks come to me because the product they had previously bought from someone else did not perform as they were promised it would. Unfortunately, by the time they came to me, it was too late to remedy the situation. Being ethical and providing the right service and product will ensure that you will have not only a fine career but a profitable one.

Sustain the Drive—Follow Through

I attribute part of my success to my ability to sustain follow-through in my business. Once I sell a policy to a client, they become part of a family of sorts, a family I vow to contact 12 times a year. Within those 12 contacts, two of these will take place first by phone and then in person when I invite my clients to meet with me to review their contracts. To do a policy review is a lot of work for my office. Why do I do all of this? The answer is simple: I care about my clients. And because I care, my average policyholder will go on to purchase insurance from me seven times in the course of their lifetime. Seven times!

In between these various purchases, I send my clients pieces of literature including a quarterly tax report and a magazine entitled *Creative Living* along with two pieces of mail. And when I say "mail," I don't mean an email but an actual personalized letter, sent with a stamp and everything. Never underestimate the power of a personalized *physical* letter. We live in a world where people no longer get actual letters. We are all bombarded by hundreds of emails a day, reducing the power of an email to zero.

I remember the time when I sent one of my clients a birthday card. Here was a gentleman who was married with two children. He called me up. "Paul," he said, "you were the only one to wish me a happy birthday this year."

That broke my heart, but it reminded me of the importance of maintaining a close relationship with clients, especially in this changing world where a married man with two kids might not have anyone wish him a happy birthday, other than his insurance agent. How sad is that?

This type of follow-through service I provide my clients not only ensures that I stay abreast of my clients' needs, but it maintains an authentic human-to-human connection that fosters long-term trust.

Most of Life Is Mundane

Let's face it. There is nothing like the thrill of making a deal, but it is important to remember that most of life is mundane. I have a theory that most people could in fact be successful if only they disciplined themselves to embrace the mundane of the day-to-day. So many people get stuck in the first phase of success when they acquire that new client or land that account. But this initial phase of a victory marks only the very beginning of the battle. I call it a *battle* because it is. When you're building a career, you're doing more than just acquiring a client here and a client there; you're building an entire lifetime of work ahead of you. Creating a career is a process that is made up of a-million-and-one tiny little steps devoid of glamour and excitement.

I love thinking about the true winners in our world and looking at how they accomplished their victories. Look at world-famous marathon swimmer Diana Nyad, who swam around Manhattan (28 miles) and from North Bimini in the Bahamas to Juno Beach in Florida (102 miles). And if those accomplishments were not enough, Diana decided she wanted to become the first person to swim from Havana to Key West unaided by a shark cage.

What is so extraordinary about Diana Nyad's story is that she did not give up on the goal to swim from Cuba to Florida, which she failed to reach at the age of 28, when she made her first attempt. Instead of giving up, Diana decided to try again when she was 60 years old! Now most of you know that professional athletes usually retire sometime in their 30s because the body cannot sustain the endurance required of that level of athleticism. So Diana did just that—she retired. But that missed goal of hers she had tried to reach at the age of 28 kept nagging at her. So when she entered the ripe old age in her sixth decade, she decided she would try again.

Coaches told her that this goal was an impossible feat for a woman her age. Doctors tried to discourage her from attempting something they told her could be fatal. Every single person in her life urged her to give up and accept the fact that she was too old and could not achieve this goal. But Diana wouldn't hear it. She set out to train for the incredible journey ahead.

What I love about Nyad's story is that she equates the journey of a life with the metaphor of a marathon swim. "The first ten hours were great!" Diana said. When she first jumped in the water and began to swim, she was enthralled by the thrill of the early phases of her battle, the thrill of the initial phases of her journey. Life is like a marathon swim: When you first start, you have the thrill of the start, the ease of each stroke as your body glides through the waters, but after a few hours, exhaustion begins to set in and challenges begin to make themselves known. When Diana was in the 24th hour of her fourth attempt at reaching her goal to swim from Cuba to Florida, she was stung by a deadly box jellyfish. These nasty little creatures kill more people than sharks, and when they inject their venom into your veins, the poison often has the effect of shutting down the involuntary reflex of breathing and your heart beating. When she was stung, the doctors injected Diana with adrenaline and with steroids and, per her request, put her back into the water to finish her journey. Isn't that what life is like? You first have the thrill of the start, and then without fail, you are faced with the challenges of the mundane. How you end up handling that part of your journey will determine whether or not you will succeed.

It was on her fifth attempt, and after facing countless challenges ranging from treacherous weather to deadly jellyfish, that

Diana Nyad succeeded in becoming the first person to swim from Havana to Key West unaided by a shark cage. She was 64 years old.

When asked how she succeeded in doing something every single person around her told her would be an impossible feat, Diana credits her success to her relentless discipline and tenacity. By "discipline," Diana means showing up day after day after day and working through the million-and-one strokes of her training. And by "tenacity" Diana means staying engaged and present in her daily work.

Diana will tell you that she never gave up, her favorite mantra being "Find a way!" The challenge is not finding a way to swim 110 miles like Diana did, but to find the courage to keep going beyond the initial and enthralling first ten hours. All in all, it took Diana 53 hours to complete her swim. Fifty-three hours where she had to continuously push through the mundane of the next stroke and the next stroke and the next, well beyond the point of excitement or thrill or joy of gliding in the waters at the start. This is how winners do it. They show up, and they show up again, and they show up again, and push through the muck of the day-to-day.

Ninety percent of the process of winning is pushing through the mundane. Can you handle it? The reality of day-to-day life requires that you make your bed, that you do the dishes, that you put them away, and that you do it all over again the next day and the next day after that. The same is true of building a career. We live in a society where everything is romanticized. Get-rich-quick scams are all over the Internet, and when you watch reality shows depicting a marriage or a business in the making, it makes it look so easy and rosy as if entire corporations were built overnight. But the reality is that whether you're starting a business or maintaining a marriage or family, it requires a-million-and-one little steps that you have to take every day. There is no glamour in those steps. From calling your potential clients, to changing diapers and doing the dishes, these tasks will never make the center of focus of prime-time television and yet, guess what? Most of work is like this. It's a lot of little things. There is nothing thrilling about these little tasks and yet, together, it is these little things that add up to extraordinary results, like being able to swim from Havana to Key West at age 64.

You Know What to Do; Now Do It

Many people squander their gifts. There are extreme cases like the famous football player Aaron Hernandez who threw it all away after being arrested for murder. What a waste of an incredible gift. There are others who are not in the limelight but for one reason or another, may it be laziness, fear, or simply lack of confidence, throw away brilliant potential. But you can't take potential to the bank. What matters in the end is what you do end up doing with your life, not what you could have done or should have done. There comes a point in everyone's life, usually at the end of your 20s, when you have to define yourself, define your dreams, and identify your goals, so you can start working each day towards bringing that vision to life.

Regardless of how old you are today, the moment for you to bring your vision to life has come. You know what you need to do, now go out and do it.

Life Lesson Moment

Take a moment to think about one of your dream goals in life. It doesn't have to be something as huge as swimming 110 miles in a shark–infested ocean. It can be something like acquiring two new clients this month or learning how to play the piano. Whatever your goal might be, write it down. Now break it down into chunks of achievable steps. If you want to learn how to play the piano at a basic level, the first step you will have to take is to find a teacher or nearby school where you can enroll to start learning. Break it down again into the smaller steps. Enroll into level 1 piano lessons. Every evening, practice playing for 30 minutes. Keep going, keep breaking it down into smaller and smaller steps until you have a list of manageable goals.

Now take a look at your list of tasks to accomplish. What does this list look like? You will notice that most of the tasks on this list are not very glamorous. The big question you will need to ask yourself is this: *Does my passion for my goal far outweigh the dulling reality of those required day-to-day tasks?* If your answer is "no," then perhaps you might want to come up with a new goal.

Do you remember waking up as a kid, bubbling with excitement for the day ahead? You were so excited that you forgot to eat or brush your teeth or take a shower. If you remember that kind of unbridled passion from your childhood, then you know that this is the kind of engagement you want to cultivate in each of your goals. Do you think that your mother stopping you from running out of the house before brushing your teeth or eating breakfast made you lose interest in that game you were going to play with your buddies later on? Doubtful. You couldn't wait to get out there and you didn't care if 22 of the 25 tasks you needed to do before you could play were tedious. You did what you needed to do so you could reach your goals. This is the kind of relentless engagement you must ask of yourself today, dear reader.

How to Build Discipline & Achieve Big Goals

Every great athlete will tell you that their victories are born out of a regimented discipline. The same is true for successful businesspeople. Make sure that you develop a deep commitment to discipline. The art of discipline is the ability to show up for yourself, your clients and your business on a consistent basis and push through the daily challenges of the mundane. Don't let boredom or complacency derail you. Move past the mundane by following these simple but important action steps.

Action Steps

Know your weakness. People often attempt to cover up any vulnerabilities or pretend they don't exist. Until you can acknowledge your shortcomings, you won't be able to overcome them. Are there habits or daily behaviors that you know slow your momentum down during the day? Are you surfing the web too often? Do you chat on the phone a little too long? Address these distractions and weaknesses so that you can approach your workday in the most efficient and streamlined way possible.

Keep it simple. Dream big but plan small. You already know from Chapter 4's tip on breaking down goals into smaller steps that the best way to get big things done is by focusing on and accomplishing the smaller steps along the way. There is no need to get bogged down and ultimately overwhelmed by the "bigness" of the end product. Do keep your eye on the prize, but don't let it paralyze you from getting it done!

Combine something you want to do with something you need to do. For tasks that you are tempted to put off, combine them with something you enjoy. For example: Listen to your favorite music while organizing your files. There is a reason why long-distance runners will play their favorite playlists while training for a long race. Think of yourself as a long-distance achiever; give yourself fuel and rewards along the way.

Remove temptations and distractions. The best strategy is "out of sight, out of mind." Toss the junk food, remove the clutter, turn off distracting media, create an environment that best allows you to get your work done and serve your clients efficiently.

Stay focused. Review your goals each morning before you start the day. Pick a quiet time or place to meditate on what you want to achieve in the short and long term. You can also write down your progress each day and acknowledge the victories along the way. This is a perfect way to acknowledge what you've accomplished so far and figure out if you need to adjust your course in order to get to the finish line on time.

Prioritize tasks. Complete the hardest and most pressing tasks first. By getting the big stressors out of the way, you will be more productive and less stressed the rest of the day. By winning the big victories first, you will give yourself the momentum to knock out everything on your list one after another.

Don't wait for it to "feel right." Once you dedicate yourself to a new disciplined routine, know that it will not feel comfortable right away. It takes on average 21 days to form a new habit, and during that time period, don't expect that you will feel comfortable in your new healthier approach to your daily work. Changing up your routine and habits can be uncomfortable and awkward at first. Embrace the feeling of "wrongness." If you're having trouble getting used to it, change a few things at a time.

Prepare a backup plan. Know what you'll say and do if temptation arises. Don't just give in the very first time you have the urge to return to your old ways. What are concrete ways you can address these inevitable moments when your old self creeps up and asks you to check your newsfeed? Having a clear, solid approach to resist your impulse to return to the old ways will make it easier to nip these bad habits in the bud and stay on course.

Get the right support. Surround yourself with people who are like-minded and supportive. There is a saying that you are a reflection of your environment. If you surround yourself with efficient and disciplined people, you will be much more apt to stay on course with your own commitment to efficiency and discipline. Take a moment to identify some blockers in your day-to-day commitment to discipline. Are there people or situations you can remove from your environment to stay on course?

Forgive yourself and move forward. Things won't always go according to plan. You're going to have ups and downs. When you have a setback, acknowledge what caused it and move on. Use the setbacks as learning experiences. Are there ways you are slowing yourself down by holding on to resentments and unaddressed feelings? Face these directly, address your shortcomings by taking actions to fix them, and forgive yourself.

CHAPTER TEN

Overcoming Hardship

L *osing your business, your job, having your clients cancel appointments, or the like—these are hardships that can be addressed and from which you can rise transformed and strengthened by your newfound wisdom.*

Life Can Change on a Dime

Nobody gets through life unscathed. Nobody has a perfect life. We all want to believe that nothing bad is going to happen to us. But the reality is that sometimes bad things do happen to good people. Over the years, I have met all kinds of people; nobody's story surprises me anymore. I've worked with most of my clients for the span of my career, providing them with many insurance contracts in the course of their lifetimes. So you can imagine that I have become close to many of them. There is nothing to prepare you for your first death claim. I love every single one of my clients, so when that first death claim hits, it doesn't feel good. And if you're in the insurance business, you will have to deal with a death claim; it is simply inevitable.

When I look back on my trajectory, I didn't know in those early years what an impact my work would have on my clients' lives. I would have really liked to have known and understood that fact earlier. This goes back to the importance of making sure that I am acquiring new clients. In my mid-career, I finally connected with the reality that when I gain a client, it is not only a commission I am gaining but also the opportunity to change and improve the lives of my clients and their children for generations to come. In all sincerity and without blurring the boundaries of humility, I can tell you that I am a life changer. I am a family saver. I wish I'd known that fact earlier on.

Never Make Assumptions

We often look at each other's lives and think the grass is greener on the other side. But the truth is that when you look at it up close, you can start discerning the presence of weeds, and all of the imperfections you could not see from where you were standing. We humans have a tendency to make assumptions about how easy or how wonderful someone else's life must be. But no matter how perfect everything seems to be on the surface, no one has everything.

Recently, Joyce and I traveled to Boston where she sits on the board of trustees at Brandeis University. We attended a function on an incredible 16-acre estate just outside of Boston owned by a wonderful couple. They have a magnificent home, two adorable girls, and upstairs, prisoner of his own mind and body, is their 19-year-old son living with cerebral palsy. Who has everything?

Sometimes life does pull the rug from under you. One afternoon you're on vacation with your wife in Mexico, getting on the treadmill for a quick jog before dinner, and the next moment you have a fatal accident, leaving your wife and children behind. That's what happened to Dave Goldberg, CEO of SurveyMonkey and husband of Sheryl Sandberg, who is the COO of Facebook. Sheryl was on vacation in Punta Mita, Mexico, with her husband, Dave, when he fell off the treadmill at the resort gym and hit his head. He died. I imagine that there is nothing that prepares you emotionally for this kind of loss. Nothing that makes it bearable for you to lose your 47-year-old husband, the father of your two small children. What a terrible thing to have happen. Life can take a brutal turn at any moment and the only thing we can do about it is to face the grief with dignity. Some things are out of your control. Death is certainly one of them.

In Judaism, when someone dies, you sit shiva for seven days, an intense period of mourning when you sit and reflect on your loss. After this seven-day period, there is another, less intense period of mourning called "sheloshim" that lasts 30 days, in which you can begin to get back to your life while still reflecting on how to face the unbearable. After her period of sheloshim for her husband's death, Sheryl Sandberg wrote a beautiful piece entitled "Let's Kick the Shit out of Option B," in which she shares some of her realizations of that terrible loss.

After her husband, Dave, died, Sheryl was trying to figure out a way to fill in for her husband when she said to a friend, "But I want Dave. I want option A," to which her friend replied, "Option A is not available. So let's just kick the sh-t out of option B."

We all need to learn to kick the sh-t out of option B, because we never know when we might need to let go of option A.

There are two types of hardships in life, the ones that engulf your life in one instant, leaving you with little or nothing to do to respond other than with absolute grief—like the death of Sheryl Sandberg's husband on that fateful vacation. And then there are those hardships that leave you with an opportunity for transformation and growth, like losing your business and filing for bankruptcy. Though terrifying and nothing short of horrible, these hardships are nothing like losing your husband or wife or child to an illness or an accident. Losing your business, your job, having your clients cancel appointments, or the like—these are hardships that can be addressed and from which you can rise transformed and strengthened by your newfound wisdom. I won't pretend I can give you any wisdom on how to face the kinds of losses that leave you with a broken heart, but I may know a thing or two about what might help you overcome and face hardships in business.

Give Back All of the Money

Several years ago, I am traveling in Lyon, France, with my wife, Joyce, feeling on top of the world. I've just sold a substantial premium to a client right before getting on the plane, and my considerable commission has freshly been deposited into my account. I am feeling relaxed and happy. When we arrive in Lyon, Joyce and I go out to dinner. We're enjoying the beautiful scenery of our European vacation when my phone rings. It's Toba, my assistant.

"I've got some bad news, Paul. It's not a good day. The client exercised their right to cancel the policy."

You see, Northwestern Mutual has a provision in their whole life contracts that allows the clients to change their mind and cancel the policy at any time during the first 11 months after purchase. So, if you're a client of mine and you decide, for whatever reason, that you don't want the product anymore, sometime within that time frame, I have to return all of your money (minus the small amount of interpolated-term cost), no questions asked. This was the second policy a client had canceled recently. I now had a substantial commission that I had to pay back to the company. This was not a good day.

I told myself, *You know what, Pauly, you're on vacation; there is nothing you can do about it. Don't worry about it. Enjoy your trip; you'll handle it when you get back. It's outside of your control; enjoy the rest of the two weeks.* And that's what I did.

When I got back, I called the company and made provisions to pay back the money over three different pay periods. I handled it, even though it was a distressing and unexpected experience. The company allowed me to return my commission over six weeks. I had two choices: move on or be a victim. I chose to move on.

Planning for the Unforeseeable Future

Here is what I learned from having to return the money: You have to plan for the unforeseeable future. Most people work thinly. They don't have huge amounts of capital and this can lead them into troubled waters. The single most important reason why small businesses don't make it during the first three years after opening is because they don't have enough capital to weather the storms. To make matters worse, we live in an economic climate that makes it difficult to borrow money from the banks. In my case with those charge backs, I was very fortunate that I was able to negotiate with Northwestern Mutual to pay the commission back over three payments. I had earned that trust with them because they knew that I was a solid asset who would continue to earn consistently. But most businesses don't have that luxury. The most common scenario is that people do not have the ability to come up with large sums of money when there is a turnaround in their business and they lose everything. I have certainly been there in the past. Right up to the point when I lost my clothing business, I had put myself into a hole by mortgaging everything, so when my business dipped significantly because of the oil crisis and the theft of my employee, I had no way out of that situation except to file for bankruptcy.

When working with small business clients, I suggest to them that they surround themselves with people who are competent in the areas that do not fall within their area of expertise, so that they can concentrate on what they do best.

The biggest problem with small companies is the lack of capitalization. A prudent businessperson should take steps to run their business, not just in good times, but during the down turns as well. Money should always be put away for contingencies, in addition to the money already allocated for technology, research, and development. The golden rule is to avoid having more than 50 percent leverage. This is a good rule of thumb, especially in the unforeseeable event that you become ill or have an accident. I remind my clients of the importance of being adequately insured in order to guarantee there is enough money in the business to avoid having to sell it in the event of a death. All businesses must be prepared, not just for the good days, but also for the downturns in the economy and in one's own health.

There Is No Such Thing as Rejection in Business

When a potential client or customer does not buy your product, they're not actually turning *you* down. There is no such thing as personal rejection in business. This is not dating. It's business. Not acquiring a client is not rejection. They don't actually know you. Maybe the timing is not right. How many times have you walked into a store and not bought something? Were you rejecting that storeowner? No. It simply wasn't the right product for you at that time. When I talk about making ten phone calls, getting three appointments, and in turn making one sale, does that mean that nine out of ten people rejected me? No.

When my client changed his mind, it dawned on me: None of this had anything to do with me. It had to do with something that had occurred in his life.

The important aspect of the challenge in this story is not having lost a commission or having to return money you thought was yours. The key question here is: How are you going to deal with this setback psychologically?

Two Types of People

Depending on your personality and the type of person you've become, you'll react in one of two ways when facing hardship. There are those who are stuck and say, *That's the end of my life. I am a victim. Look what happened to me. The client changed her mind. That's it. My career is over.* And then there is the person who says, *It's a challenge. It's a speed bump. Am I going to allow this to end my life? No!*

I have met people who when they hit a wall simply stopped moving forward. People for whom that challenge marked the end of the line. But ultimately, everyone has a choice when they hit a wall. Again, it's a conscious decision to ask yourself, *What am I going to do?* Nothing. Look at what happened to me. It has always baffled me when I've come across people who react with the deer-in-the-headlights approach to hardship.

Chances are that if you're reading this book, you're a go-getter who wants to learn to roll with the punches along the way. But in case you fall into the latter category of paralyzed people, I am here to tell you that the outcome of choosing that alternative does not end well.

Years ago, a Northwestern Mutual agent I knew was not making spectacular sums of money but he was doing just fine, working good hours and earning a respectable living. Then one day, he sells his first significant contract ever. Of course he is happy. This is great. This is his first taste at taking his career to the next level of financial success. But alas, seven months later—well within the 11-month time frame allotted to cancel a purchased policy—the client changes his mind. Guess what? It crushes this agent. He can't handle it. He quits and never sells insurance again. Don't let this happen to you. Dust yourself off and move on.

Safety Net? What's That?

Remember that there is no safety net when you're running your own business. Sure, you can put certain things in place to help cushion the blows that will inevitably come your way, but there is no actual safety net. Isn't that true of life itself? Do you think there was an emotional safety net for me when I was 29 years old and I received the news that my mother had just died during heart surgery?

When setbacks like having a client or two or three change their mind happen, it can be tough financially. But the genuine difficulty is the flood of emotions that come with that experience.

When I received the news in Lyon that my clients had changed their minds, I was upset. Of course, anger is a secondary emotion and I was probably feeling a dose of fear behind it all, but the important thing is that I did not let this fear paralyze me. Here we were, staying at a great hotel, sitting at one of those beautiful verandas, drinking champagne; I hung up the phone and just went back to our table and took another sip of champagne. This was just another *thing* that happened outside of my control. Unlike the agent who quit his job because his first big client changed his mind, I kept moving forward. That's the only viable option. And yet for some reason, that's not the only option people choose when hardship knocks on their door. You can't let life stop you in your tracks, otherwise you won't do anything.

When It Rains It Pours

By now you know that setting up appointments is the foundation of how I bring in more clients for myself. I always have a lot of appointments. If I don't have appointments, I don't have any business. One Monday, I come into the office feeling pretty energized and ready for my seven or eight appointments of the day. I say hi to my assistant and she tells me, "Everything's been canceled for today."
"Everything?" I ask, incredulous.
"Yes, each and every single one of the appointments has been canceled."
"Okay. I'll go and book more appointments."
I think to myself, *That's a little strange.* But then the next day comes and I realize, it's not as strange as the next day when it happens again on Tuesday. Which is almost as strange except that the exact thing happens again on Wednesday. And by Thursday when it happens again, I think, *That's not good.* By Friday, I don't even open the door to my office. I just slide under it. It was just one of those weird things.

Here's the fact: The world is not fair. The world is not sitting waiting to grace me. I have to admit that for a while after this fiasco happened, I was almost paralyzed. I understand how easy it is to stay down when something like this happens to you. I remember thinking to myself, *Oh my God, what happened? Why don't they want to see me?*

In facing this type of situation, which kind of person are you going to be? The person who brushes himself or herself off and gets back up without internalizing this setback as being a personal rejection or the person who stays down and becomes temporarily or even permanently paralyzed?

When the Road Gets Rocky

Years ago, while vacationing in the Bahamas, we're having lunch at a restaurant with my brother and sister-in-law. My brother is looking at the menu and orders one of these triple-layered club sandwiches. He says to the waitress, "Can you make this sandwich using lobster instead of bacon, please?" Not a big request given there is lobster everything all over the menu.

We wait and wait and wait. The sandwich doesn't come. Where's the sandwich? As it turns out, our waitress Jane—who had never been asked to change something on the menu before—went into the kitchen, freaked out, and went home! Nobody had ever asked her for that custom order before, so she went home! This is an example of a type of person out there who just gives up when they don't know what to do.

There are lots of people who, given the opportunity, would live my life in a heartbeat. People who think, *I want Paul's life*, but they don't want to do what needs to be done. They think it's going to be just smooth sailing. The first time the road gets really rocky, many give up. You can't just give up because things don't go your way.

Here is the thing about rocky roads: They are everywhere. Lots of streets have potholes—there is nothing smooth in life. Nobody has it easy. Remember that nobody goes through life unscathed. Nobody! We can't look at another person's life and say, "Wow, what a great life they have." Because the second you scratch below the surface, you find out they are struggling with something you never even imagined. They don't have a *great* life. What they have is a life they made. It might be a great life for them, but they too have issues like the rest of us.

I'll never forget a certain bump in the road in my third year in the insurance business. I hired an executive assistant to work in the office. Every day when I come in, I notice that her desk is perfectly clean. I think to myself, *Wow, this is terrific. This is a very efficient woman.*

One day I come in and tell my assistant, "So-and-So never received all of the information they requested from me. What happened?" Immediately, she gets incredibly flustered and blurts out, "I have to leave." She gets up and she leaves.

Puzzled by this behavior, I go into her desk, where I find piles upon piles of uncompleted work. Suddenly I realize that every day, she would come in to work and if there was something that she did not understand or complete, she would give up and throw the files into the desk drawer, unfinished. All of the projects and tasks I had naively assumed had been completed were now crumpled at the bottom of her desk.

Even more disturbing than her unfinished work hidden in the desk, I find snippets of her own hair she had cut and placed in one of the drawers!

I couldn't believe it.

Overnight, I woke up to a complete situation of chaos. I now had to call all of the clients she was working with at that time and tell the truth about this assistant.

What have I learned from this experience? I have learned that I did not have enough knowledge at that point in time to know that I needed to have a meeting with my assistant. And she did not have the courage to come to me and say, "Look, I am falling behind; I need your help." It is important to stay engaged with employees. Not because they are not to be trusted, but because this should be a collaborative effort with regular meetings. Had I done that, she might have found the courage to say to me that she was falling behind and that she needed my help.

By the time I hired my next assistant, who would end up working with me for 38 years, I knew enough to hold regular meetings with her so we could go over the various projects on our plate.

One thing is for sure: I'll never forget that day when I opened that drawer and it was full of hair!

Don't Fall Prey to Complacency

There are many different types of challenges and setbacks that will come your way. You don't have to reach rock bottom like I did when I filed for bankruptcy in order to be facing hardship in your career. One of the challenges that can threaten the vitality of an even well-established business is the typical slump that can occur after a few years of operation.

Have I ever been in a slump? Sure I have. The most significant slump in my career occurred when I was already well established. This is a typical development in many people's careers. If we look at the various passages of a person's life, youth is the time for experimentation. It is the optimal time to take as many risks as possible. Not only because there is less to lose, but also because the self is forming during those early years. But as time goes by, and certainly by the midpoint of a person's professional development, a kind of complacency can threaten to set in. This is a great danger. Many business professionals fall into the throws of complacency and think, *I have enough clients. I don't need to advertise. I don't need to reach out to new clients anymore.* The overconfidence that usually comes in that phase of your career can lead you to think that you're now beyond having to work for new clients. This is the type of complacency that can dangerously make you think that you don't need to rely on your old clients to get new ones.

Another danger of complacency is not staying abreast of what is going on in your occupation. I've never stopped educating myself. I always tell everybody, "Knowledge is power." The more I know about the insurance industry, the better I can serve my clients. If I give you knowledge, it enhances your life, in a way. If you buy that Ford Fusion, don't you want that salesperson to have the knowledge to answer all of your questions about your new car? Don't you want your doctor to be board certified and have to gain the validation of their peers through the mechanism of continuing education?

In my profession, I have to continue to learn so I can be a better financial planner. As an insurance professional, it is my job to give you the knowledge and the tools so that if your spouse dies, you have the option of continuing to run your life and business in the manner that you have been accustomed. My knowledge and my expertise offer you the option to do that.

Of course, whenever I meet with clients, I occasionally have questions that do stump me and where I have to say, "Wow, nobody has ever asked me that question; let me get back to you tomorrow." Absolutely. I don't believe in winging it. Once you give a client the wrong information, you jeopardize their trust. In the long run, it is best to empower yourself with information, so that you have options.

Regardless of the industry you're in, change is constant, requiring you to gain new skills and new information. Take the automobile industry. Today our cars are actually computers. When the salesperson delivers the car, they no longer hand you a key. Instead, we press a start button.

The key to a successful business is to be aware at all times of the changes that are taking place. You must have the knowledge to understand that life and business are changing around you. Take the time to learn how new technology can enhance your professional journey. Allow this process to be a joy because knowledge should be the thrill of your life and give you the power to move up to do what you want to do.

The goal is to reach the end of your professional journey and be able to say, *I am now an expert in my field. I know what I am doing. I have done 5,000 knee surgeries. I have written 5,000 insurance policies. I have sold 5,000 cars or 5,000 homes. I am good. Now, people are looking to me and they are seeking information from me. Young people are coming to me to learn from my expertise. The smart ones are at least, because they have witnessed my success and are looking up at me sitting there at the top of the mountain.*

The Glass Is Half Full — You Must Move Forward

As you can see, everyone at some point in their life is going to hit a wall or face hardship. It is inevitable. You may not be able to avoid it, but you can certainly control how you choose to face these hardships. One of the best ways to get out of a slump is to focus on what you have. "The glass is half full" sort of philosophy will push you forward to capitalize on your existing assets and skills. Even when the time comes when you will have moved past that slump, you will still need to go and visit your old clients and ask for their help to get new introductions. If you're a cardiologist, you have to contact a lot more internists to get new patients. You might be facing the challenge of falling out of favor with some of your previous clients, or your industry might be undergoing a major change not in your control. Whatever the case may be, you always have the option of building upon what you have already built and solidifying your business by maximizing the assets you already have.

Broaden Your Horizon

Something radical changed in my own business when I was in my 40s: The medical industry changed with the advent of the preferred provider organization or PPO. This impacted the careers of doctors tremendously and they went from making $1–2 million a year to $400,000. Doctors were my primary clients in those earlier years, and seemingly overnight, their incomes were slashed. Suddenly, Medicare said, "Listen, Mr. Ophthalmologist, you're getting $2,500 for a cataract surgery; now we're going to pay you only $400."

Up until that point, doctors represented a large segment of my clients, but when their market changed, I realized I had to change mine as well and went on to expand my clientele to include business managers in Hollywood. Your clientele may not be doctors or the entertainment industry, but I can guarantee you that there is or will be an equivalent change that is or will take place in your own industry. The key here is to maintain the ability to remain flexible and weather the changes that come your way.

When I took that five-week vacation—one week for each of the decades of my life up to that point—I took stock on how successful my career had become. I reveled in the fact that life is made up of all of these wonderful challenges and hidden opportunities. But I know that it didn't just happen overnight or on its own. I worked to make this success happen. I faced my own insecurities and made the most of what I already had. I did not allow external circumstances to define me nor did I let my own insecurities paralyze me. There were many times when I thought that people were smarter than me. And guess what? Sometimes they were, but they did not have my skills in communications. There are many people who are much smarter than I am. But what I have is great knowledge and wisdom in my chosen field and the ability to think on my feet. This is a skill that you can adapt for your own career. That goes back to that presentation I gave in that conference room facing Mount Rainier. I turned that situation around so that the potential clients would pay attention to me instead of the majestic mountain just beyond the window.

Recognize the skills that you do have; make the most of them and don't worry about the people who are smarter than you. Nothing can be gained from focusing your energy on things you cannot change. People have different skills. Focusing on such things is not productive.

There have been times in my life when I was slowed down by obstacles or challenges, but I have never been paralyzed, except when I was held at gunpoint. If you are going to own your life, then you're not going to be a victim. Instead of reveling in your own failures, I would suggest reveling in your successes and focusing on what you have instead of what you don't have. Why not say, "This is my success." Once you have basked in your accomplishments, keep on going. Don't stop!

Embrace Change

One of the most beautiful things about life is that it is always in a state of flux. Change is what makes our existence so interesting. Do not think, *Oh my gosh, my client base is gone because the laws changed.* Instead, think, *Wow, how lucky am I that I now get to meet all sorts of new people.* Stay positive at all times.

These types of changes don't just represent a challenge, but they are simply a part of life. It's part of keeping yourself alive and making yourself vibrant. Look at me now. I'm 78 years old. Each day offers brand new opportunities. I'm continuously expanding my horizons. The key is to develop such a whole and complete sense of self that no circumstance or external change is going to destroy you.

Recently, I ran into a doctor at the gym who used to perform the insurance medical exams for client policies. He is retired now. I went up to him and we started chatting, and within a few seconds of our exchange, he shares with me that now that he is retired, he feels like a complete failure. "I don't have patients who need me anymore," he tells me. "And when I do run into a former patient, they hardly acknowledge me. They just don't need me." I feel bad for the guy. Not because his ex-patients don't say "hi" to him but because he has allowed himself to be defined by external circumstances and by the inevitable changes that come along in the course of a lifetime.

Recently, I semi-retired. Even though I no longer go into an office every day, I am still as busy as ever. My day-to-day activities may have changed, but my passion and engagement for life have not. I certainly do not allow my age to be a deterrent to the excitement I feel about everything I still do today. When I look back on my life, I realize that it is a continuum. I know where I've been, what I did, and where I want to go from here.

The circumstances of your life are going to continuously change. If you're fortunate enough to have kids and have them go off to college, they will leave you and your partner to face a new phase of your lives. Are you going to feel like your life is now empty and purposeless because your nest is empty, or are you going to face that change and say, "What a great opportunity for me and my spouse to discover that new chapter of our lives"?

If you get fired, lose your business, or whatever the change or challenge you might be facing, it will have one thing to offer you: an opportunity to get honest with yourself and make some changes. The key during this time of transformation is to watch your business take on a new dimension as you move towards new opportunities. If the business that you're in is not going to work, move on. Don't get stuck. Be honest. Look at the full picture.

How Much Are You Willing to Put into It?

The interesting thing about success is that the solutions to the challenges are not complicated. If you want to make it happen, then you have to take the good with the bad and the bad with the good. At the end of the day, it's all about how much energy you are willing to expend and what you're willing to put into it.

I saw a cartoon once that struck me so much that it never faded from my memory. The drawing represents a man in a bookstore perusing the shelves, when he comes upon a title that reads *How to Make a Million Dollars*. The book costs $1. A few feet away, the man comes upon a second book with another title: *How to Make Two Million Dollars*. And that book costs $2. Unfortunately, I don't recall the illustrator of that cartoon but I remember its message, which is simple. If you're willing to put $2 instead of $1 into the purchase of a book, then you stand to gain twice as much. The more energy you put into something, the more you gain.

When it comes to manifesting success and you're looking for answers, the answers are right there in front of you. They are not deep answers. If you're looking for a deep answer, then you're looking for an excuse to not do the work. The bottom line is this: If you're selling Samsung and suddenly LG and GE come out with competing appliances, you have to find a better product and educate the public on how much better yours is. That's what you do. Period. Remember Diana Nyad and her goal of swimming from Havana to Key West? What would have happened if she had listened to the naysayers in her life and given up on her goal? What would have happened if she had stopped after her first attempt 35 years earlier? Don't let yourself or anyone else tell you that you will do anything less than that.

We Are Not Born Equal

Whether we like to admit it or not, we are not born equal. I know this sounds awful. Some people have the innate talent to be neurosurgeons while others do not. But more importantly, not everyone picks up after a terrible fall. When I look back on those people like that waitress who went home after she received an unusual order, I realize that some people just don't make it after a terrible blow. Not everyone is Peyton Manning with the ability to retrain himself after a terrible neck injury. But those who seek and are curious will fight and they will get back up.

Every great hero is flawed with the liabilities of their past. My father was not a good role model. Was that going to make me a victim? I had a lot to overcome. Was I going to blame it on those early years in my life? What was I going to do with that baggage? Transform it and make it something worthwhile, or blame every setback? The countless gray areas of our lives make for powerful opportunities for growth and forgiveness. Even though I grew up hearing negative comments about myself, I was not going to let that be an impediment to my growth and success. Who can say, without hesitation, that they are not flawed? I certainly cannot. The only thing that matters in rising from the ashes is the decision to move beyond victimhood into the fullness of the circumstances that have made us who we are today. It is the courage to do so—not the absence of his flaws—that marks the distinction of a great hero.

Some people move forward and some people get stuck and become victims. My brother and I had a disappointing father. When I was a kid, I had a lisp, and my father used to make fun of me. He'd go, "Thay, what did you think of that?" He'd pick on all my "Ss." I'd say, "Tuesday," and he'd repeat, "Tuethday." Then he would say, "What are you? Stupid?" I could either tell myself that I was worthless or choose to move forward and build something out of my life. Believe me, we did not live in opulence. I mean, I lived on Overland Avenue for Pete's sake. Look where Sotomayor came from; she lived in the projects. John Boehner worked in his father's bar. You can't change your origins. Many people give in to their insecurities; they allow their setbacks to keep them from ever moving forward. There are great athletes who walk off the field after their last game or performance marking the end of their life because they are unable to reinvent themselves.

When I went bankrupt, what an opportunity. I was finally able to look at my own failures and recognize that I needed to get serious.

The American Dream Is Bigger Than Ever

People who have faced too many hardships and have not managed to get back up believe that the American Dream is gone. But the American Dream is bigger and more expansive than it ever was. Today, we have young people at 15 years of age who design apps on their own and become billionaires. People who don't believe in the American Dream are just searching for excuses they can pull out of their bag as to why they're not making something out of their life. The American Dream is still possible.

Look at the Blue Star Mothers of America, launched by a small group of parents who wanted to provide support to mothers with sons and daughters in active service in the U.S. Armed Forces. This organization is a perfect example of ingenuity and the birth of a service born out of conviction. Originally formed during World War II, families of servicemen would hang a Service Flag in a window of their homes. The flag had one star for each family member in the military. If the serviceman was living, the star was blue, and if it was gold, it meant the serviceman had lost his life. In 2011, membership to the Blue Star Mothers was extended to include not just sons and daughters, but stepchildren and foster children. The service was not only for biological mothers but for adoptive mothers, foster mothers, female guardians, and grandmothers as well. The people who founded this organization were driven by the dream of helping other parents like themselves. Great innovation and change always comes out of need fueled by passion and a vivid dream waiting to be brought to life.

Good Luck, Bad Luck, No Luck

I could not write a chapter about overcoming hardship without discussing the elusive topic of luck. What is luck? How do we go about getting it? Are we equal when it comes to luck? I have noticed that there are three manifestations of luck in life—good, bad, and no luck. Good luck is that mystical alignment of perfect circumstances. Like when you run into Joe at the gym and he gives you the card for a referred client and you end up making the deal the very next day. Good luck is having only five minutes to spare for your biggest meeting of the year because you were caught in traffic but then landing a perfect parking spot in front of the office where your meeting is held. I have had my share of good luck in my life. Certainly landing that first big client early on in my insurance career was great luck.

It's going to Vegas and putting $1,000 on green and *BAM*, winning a ton of money.

Bad luck, unlike no luck, happens directly to you. It's that dark cloud following the cartoon character Joe Btfsplk in *Li'l Abner* and bringing calamity wherever he goes. Getting hit by a car is bad luck, unless you were standing in the middle of the street for hours on end. Bad luck is when your brand-new puppy nips a man at the beach who happens to be the biggest dog bite lawyer in the county.

Most of life is no luck. You don't know if you're lucky or not lucky. No luck is that neutral zone between good and bad luck. It is life in the mundane, the in-between moments between the great and terrible things happening in your life. So no luck is just the day-to-day. In order to understand "no luck," I use a golf analogy. Most golfers are just duffers. You try to get here, you try to get there, and most of the time your golf level is just ho-hum. Nothing special to write home about. If you think about it, only 2 percent of golfers ever break 100. It's a tough game. But all of a sudden, you hit that ball, and it makes that sweet sound. And wow. There is that perfect moment when you can finally watch the ball fly through the air and land perfectly. *That* moment is why people play golf. All they want, all any of us ever want, whether we play golf or not, is to hear that sweet, sweet sound. But for the rest of the time, we're all out there fumbling around in the sand, working away at making the next shot happen. The easiest way to think about luck is to realize that good luck differentiates bad luck by going to the city of no luck.

If you're a self-employed person out there in the trenches and you're working very hard to get business, you're going to acquire a client who is very affluent. That client will be somewhat of a life-changer for you. It's going to make a big difference in your income. Is that lucky? I believe you make your own luck. The reality is that you've been working hard. You're on the phone. You're out there. You're networking. You're putting yourself in the right places to meet people. You're asking to meet new clients and referrals for new clients. You're making a name for yourself. If you talk and see enough people, you'll run into somebody who will change your life.

But hard work alone is not enough; you also need to work strategically. In other words, you need to work smart. This means that you're aiming to connect with those who have the right income capacity to be a good client. If you're a lawyer, they can afford your fees. If you're a car salesman, they're going to buy that expensive car, or maybe buy two cars. You're putting yourself in the public eye in such a manner that eventually you'll run into somebody who will be that special client, who will change the direction of your practice. If you're out there doing these things, you're going to have some good luck because you're putting yourself in a position to have good luck. So success is a combination of smart and hard work and good luck.

I've often asked myself if luck is a random cycle that moves through our lives like a storm. I believe that luck runs cyclically. There are people and circumstances that defy the odds. We can't change some events in our lives, but we can change how we react. We make or break our luck by putting ourselves in positions where we can find opportunities.

A lucky Virginia couple named Calvin and Zatera Spencer won the lottery three times in a month, becoming instant millionaires. There was also Angelo and Maria Gallina who won the California lottery twice on the same day, beating the one in twenty-four TRILLION chances to do so. What do we make of luck? We work hard to make it go our way, and we buy the ticket!

A lot of times, we make our luck in business. If you're referred to a large successful firm and you do your homework and follow through on all of the required steps to stay on top of the process of acquiring that client, guess what? You'll win the competition. The only way to make your own luck is by developing a rock-solid work ethic.

I love the story of the small parish priest who prays every night that he will win the lottery so he can help his parishioners who are among the poorest in the country. Each night, the priest gets on his knees and prays: "Lord Jesus, please help me." And each day, he doesn't win the lottery. Finally, one night as he is getting ready to get down on his knees to pray again, he hears a blaring voice come down from way above in the clouds: "BUY A TICKET!"

This joke sums up my philosophy on luck. Yes, I think prayer is a beautiful thing, but ultimately, I think it's important to buy a ticket. It is important to recognize the streaks of luck in our lives. Gratitude for all of the wonderful things we do goes a long way. I know a man whose 21-year-old son was killed on his motorcycle on his way to school. That, without a doubt is very bad luck.

The Power of Resiliency

You can't avoid hardship but you can either get up or off your behind and go out and do it, or just give up. One of my clients had his biggest customer not pay him a substantial amount of money, and he went bankrupt. He didn't get a penny, and just like that, it was game over for him. Everybody in business has hard knocks. And the hardships extend themselves to every industry and profession. Do you think that the president of this country wants to get out of bed every day? I am sure that the day the Iraqi city of Ramadi fell to ISIS was not a great day for the president. But he kept moving forward.

The real question is whether or not you are resilient enough to bounce back from your troubles. Since you're holding this book in your hand, I am betting by now that you might have the willingness to apply one of these tips to your own life in order to explore your ability to bounce back.

Take Three Steps Back to Travel a Mile Forward

There are times in life when it is important to find the courage to take three steps back in order to travel a mile forward. I know the story of two different doctors who had terrible setbacks occur in their respective careers, requiring them to change the course of their career completely. The first doctor was a surgeon who developed terrible arthritis in his hands. The excruciating pain in his hands made it impossible for him to continue his practice performing difficult surgeries. The second doctor was a neurosurgeon I knew who developed a non-Parkinson's related palsy in his hands. Once again, it was no longer possible for this neurosurgeon to go on. What did they each do? Both of them chose to become malpractice attorneys. Talk about creative reinvention. Each of these people took a terrible setback and took three steps back. Was going back to law school a risk? Absolutely! Was interrupting that large income a temporary setback? You bet! Did these changes require sacrifices? Absolutely! But do you know what happened and where they are today? Each of these former surgeons cannot fulfill the number of clients that are beating a path to their door.

In the case of these two people, hardship had hit them and they had no choice but to find a new way to earn a living. But I have an example of someone who did just that without facing a terrible hardship. Many years ago, an estate-planning attorney on the Westside of Los Angeles refers one of his clients to me. The client needed a fairly extensive estate plan and it turns out that the client needed a substantial amount of life insurance to go along with it. When it was all said and done, the insurance agent's commission was significantly higher than that made by the attorney who thought, *Perhaps maybe now is the time for me to take a risk, reevaluate my career, and make a career change. I can use my skills and education to increase my income substantially.* Guess what the attorney did? He decided to take a risk, reconfigure his life, and become a Northwestern Mutual insurance person. Today, he is an enormously successful insurance agent with great expertise as a tax attorney. He is getting referrals from other attorneys who know that he is an expert who can be trusted. Today, he is a highly respected professional, both in the legal and insurance fields.

Life Lesson Moment

When you reach the end of the line, as I did in August of 1974, don't look at yourself as a failure. Life is full of changes and challenges; the key is to embrace them. My uncle Howard was married to a woman whose father owned a bingo parlor on the boardwalk in Santa Monica. The city had to close him down because games of that nature were illegal back then. He never regained his momentum. Closing the bingo parlor crushed him.

Dear reader, I am talking to you right now, especially if you're debating whether or not you should quit moving forward. I am talking to anyone out there who might be saying or thinking, *It wasn't my fault I didn't make this sale or I didn't get that job. It was because of my dad or my mom or my upbringing.* To anyone out there thinking these words, I would like to ask you this: Are you ready to take responsibility for your life and recognize that all that matters is what you're going to do about the predicament you're in today so that you can change it NOW?

Let me ask you this: *What do you envision for yourself? Is it time for a change in your life? Think of hardship as the opportunity you've been waiting for to move yourself out of that slump.* Now all of these excuses you've been telling yourself for the past several years, they don't even exist anymore. Move forward. As Diana Nyad would say: Find a way!

How to Deal with Rejection

Ultimately, there is no such thing as rejection in business. In reality: How can a person reject me if they don't know me? When you are in the public sphere and calling people for appointments, their *no* is not a form of rejection. It only means that person isn't ready for the services you're offering them. Don't take it personally. This is business, not a marriage. And remember that timing is everything. When you choose one car over another when making a purchase at a dealership, you're not actually rejecting the salesperson. You're simply making a choice more appropriate for you. Don't waste your time feeling sad or angry when something does not go your way. It's not about you.

Action Steps

Keep showing up. Don't quit after a rejection. In the same line as keeping track of your victories, keep track of your efforts at reaching your goal. Do not allow yourself to get discouraged by a mere *no*. Remember that just because you're not instantly great at something does not mean you should give it up. Regroup and find an improved way to do it again. "Sticktoitiveness" is an underrated life skill.

Acknowledge your disappointment. Sure, you are going to feel some emotions when you get that no. But don't waste any time wallowing in your feelings of anger. Take a moment, feel it, breathe, and then move on.

Assess who you really are. It's hard to take an honest look at yourself, but you need to be totally aware of your capabilities and your weak spots, instead of being surprised by the outcome. Not everyone can be a pro baseball player or a great musician. That doesn't mean you can't push your own limits and become the best you can be. After any life rejection, keep it in perspective—especially if you were not quite ready for that more ambitious goal. Take some time to regroup and prepare yourself for the next bar of achievement. You can do it!

You are more powerful than you think. Most people underestimate themselves greatly and never tap into their full potential. Remind yourself that with enough focused work, you can perform better and become better. Make a list of all of the ways that you are powerful, skilled, and able and connect these abilities to specific goals you are aiming to reach.

Commit to always being well prepared and doing your best. Success demands efficient work. If you want it, you have to put in the hours, so you can master the skills you need to compete. And then, you have to show up wholeheartedly anytime you need to perform. Are there areas of your business where you feel you could be better prepared? Set aside time each week for self-improvement and gaining additional skills under your belt.

Don't let it define you. You're not a loser or a failure just because you didn't land the client. Make sure you don't internalize the losses and failures. We've already established that these external circumstances do not define you. Each experience is an opportunity to hone your skills for the next challenge and to learn from your mistakes. Make a list of ways you could have done things differently now that you have the benefit of hindsight 20/20 vision. Learn the lessons, improve your approach moving forward, and move on.

Expect to be rejected again. Rejection isn't pleasant, but it's an inevitable part of life. If you know it's a constant possibility, it becomes far less threatening. Once you really understand that these inevitable *noes* do not define you, then you will be able to better accept them in the future. Do take the opportunity to learn from not landing a client. Ask yourself: *Is this the right client for me or do I want/need to adjust my course?* If it is the right client, meaning that it is a client you can truly serve well, then are there ways you can improve your approach with future potential clients? If this is not the most realistic client for you right now, are there skills you still need to learn or ways you can polish yourself before you can get a *yes* from the same type of client? As always, take the time to learn from this situation. Ultimately, make sure that you are seeing and talking to enough potential clients. Eventually, you will get a *yes*.

PART THREE

The Need for Love and a Sense of Belonging

When I found out that Steve Jobs passed away, my first thought was: I wonder if he would have liked me. *This tells you a lot about me and how I think. I was not thinking about the impact of his accomplishments or the products of his genius but rather about how the two of us would have related to each other. The element I value most in business is the forging of relationships.*

CHAPTER ELEVEN

The Power of Relationships

*T*he element I value most in business is the forging of relationships. Young businesspeople often focus so hard on all of the steps they need to take to build a successful business that they might overlook the simplest and most important steps: cultivating relationships and getting referred leads.

Maslow will tell you that once you've mastered the ability to find food, shelter, and create security for yourself and your family, you will have freed up energy to focus on your relationships and your need for love and a sense of belonging. No matter how you slice it, we humans are social animals whose thirst for connection drives much of our efforts beyond our basic push to survive.

When I found out that Steve Jobs passed away, my first thought was: *I wonder if he would have liked me.* This tells you a lot about me and how I think. I was not thinking about the impact of his accomplishments or the products of his genius but rather about how the two of us would have related to each other. The element I value most in business is the forging of relationships. Young businesspeople often focus so hard on all of the steps they need to take to build a successful career that they might overlook the simplest and most important steps: cultivating relationships and getting referred leads. Of course, you can't have referred leads without a solid foundation of successful client relationships.

Don't Write Me a Check

Here I am, working for decades with this great big company Northwestern Mutual. But the whole time, I am convincing clients to work with *me*, the human being, not the company. Yes, of course, I represent the product, but ultimately, the people trust *me*, the person. It is an interesting paradigm to represent a company, but you can do it effectively only by filtering it through a powerful and successful person-to-person relationship. The impact of this paradigm is especially apparent in the early phase of a client relationship, when trust has not yet been firmly established.

One day, the CEO of a large corporation in California purchased a substantial retirement program from me for one of the corporation's top-tier people. During the course of the process of working with this client, I had established a relationship with the executives of the company based on trust. When the moment came for us to send them a statement for the first annual premium, outlining the amount of money to be paid each year, we clearly stated who the check should be made payable to. Yet, when we received the check in the mail, it was not written to Northwestern Mutual but to me personally. Of course I sent it back. But the point of this anecdote is that the company was so comfortable with the work I had done with them that they wrote the check to me directly. The cornerstone of a successful business is relationships.

How Many Cars Do Robots Purchase?

Walter Reuther, who was the president of the United Automobile Workers—one of the largest unions in the U.S.—was visiting a GM plant, years ago. The president of GM took Walter on a tour, showing him all of the automated processes they were using. The president said to Walter, "We have really modernized everything. We have eliminated overhead. Isn't this fantastic? What do you think?"

Walter replied, "I have never seen anything like this in my life. It's unbelievable to see how machines are taking over. I have one question to ask you, however."

"What's that?" asked the president of GM.

"How many cars do robots purchase?" Walter replied.

No matter how efficient your business becomes, its heart lies with people and not with technology as a stand-in for human connection.

Many businesses today are using tools and know-how as a stand-in for human-to-human contact. We have all had the miserable experience of trying to book a reservation on an airline using an automated system or calling our phone carrier to resolve a billing issue only to hear the non-tonal automated voice at the other end of the line. Who wants to scream, "Representative! *Representative!*" over and over again into the phone? I am not against technology, nor do I believe that it is mutually exclusive with the forging of relationships. In fact, I would say that technology is a great tool to enhance the foundation that you have already built through face-to-face interactions. But when these tools become a stand-in for human contact, we're in trouble.

One of my clients was always requesting information regarding his policies. He would call me often and ask to get basic figures about his account. In the old days, I'd have to fish the answers and get back to him within a day or two. Today, my client can go online and instantly access this type of information himself. This is a perfect use of our current technology. I still have a relationship with my client and it was built over time. It was built through face-to-face contact. You know that you're using technology effectively when it becomes a tool that amplifies rather than replaces you. Personally, my relationships with my clients have remained strongly intact; I have not allowed technology to take the place of real human contact, but instead it has enriched the process I have built in the "real" world.

There are many ways in which technology can be used to *enhance* but not *replace* the human interaction at hand. For example, when you're about to meet with a prospective client, you can Google them or vice versa, allowing you to gain additional information about one another. You can use technology to sharpen your focus with your target audience and reach out to a larger client base within the demographics you are targeting. Once you have built trust with someone through direct contact, you can establish additional contact via Skype or FaceTime in order to help maintain the connection and to exchange information. These are all effective uses of technology as enhancements, but the moment this process takes the place of the actual human connection, you know you're in troubled waters.

When you're interested in purchasing a house, you can go online and do a virtual tour. But can you gain a *feel* for this home online? Can you really get a clear sense of what this dwelling is like without actually setting foot inside it? I don't think so.

There have been amazing inventions with the advent of developing technology and these innovations are not slowing down one bit in our current society. Apple announced they will launch their first electric car by 2019. Talk about reinventing yourself—they have strategically decided that their existing knowledge and expertise with software and batteries is a great platform to foray into the automobile industry. Only time will tell as far as determining whether they succeed or not. Apple is not the only innovator. Google and Tesla have formed a partnership to develop self-driving cars. Will this invention benefit us as a society? Will it set us back, both practically but also as social animals? It's too soon to say. Steven Shladover, manager of the UC Berkeley California Partners for Advanced Transportation Technology (PATH), believes in the project when he announced that "It's not a technology for the sake of technology. It can help us alleviate congestion; it can help reduce energy use and emissions."[1]

Ultimately, the development and use of new technologies should be about progress. Isn't that what we want? Things to move forward. But what about the possible diminishing power of human contact?

---

1   http://www.greenbiz.com/article/apple-google-tesla-and-race-electric-self-driving-cars

Does technology connect or alienate us from one another? That's a big question. Technology is a tool that can enhance a process, but it's the human being that makes it happen.

I personally struggle with technology. I don't like having to troubleshoot technical issues on my own. I dislike it when I try to accomplish a task and a technical glitch gets in the way of my own productivity. Most recently, I have been experiencing problems with my printer. When this kind of challenge happens, I seek the help of a tech-savvy person who can help me.

What is the sweet spot between technology being an enhancing factor, rather than an alienating one? There is a fine balance between the two. I am not sure I can actually answer that question. But I will tell you two stories about the priceless value of excellent service provided by an actual person.

Recently, I found that I cannot pair my computer with my existing printer. The printer is old and the computer is new. I called HP and I asked to talk to the tech person because I am not even sure how to ask the questions about the computer. He did not want to connect me with a technician and hung up on me. I was not rude or short with him; I was very quiet and patient. There really was no reason for him to hang up. And yet, he could not process my request and disconnected me. I called the HP sales teams numerously, and every single time I've been unable to reach an actual person and have been connected to a robotic automated message that runs in a loop. This is a perfect example of that point where technology has become alienating and actually sets us back instead of helping us accomplish a particular task or solving a problem.

Here's the thing: It appears that large companies simply don't want to spend the money on having actual human contact solve their customers' problems. Instead they are replacing the humans with automation in the hopes of saving money. But guess how much this is actually costing them? A frustrated customer is not a returning customer. Isn't that more costly than anything?

Caring Is Succeeding

There is an iconic restaurant in the Vail valley called Sweet Basil. I went there several years ago with some friends. This is a place that prides itself on dedication, innovation, and hard work. So, I go there with our friends, and Richard orders a steak for dinner, medium rare. The steak comes. We are enjoying ourselves. Richard takes his knife, cuts into the meat, and it is well done. He calls the waiter over. Within 90 seconds, he had another steak on his plate, this time perfectly medium rare. Ninety seconds. That's all it took for them to bring another steak. By the end of the meal and given how smooth the resolution to this issue had been, we had all forgotten about the incident. Nobody remembered that he had to wait 90 seconds for his steak. They bring the check over and the waiter says, "We did not charge you for your steak." That right there is good business. If you think about it from a business standpoint, this restaurant *lost* the cost of a steak but they *gained* a highly satisfied and impressed customer for life. Would you spend the cost of a steak to do that? I would! It's cheaper and more efficient to retain happy existing customers than to cultivate and find new ones. Now when I think of that restaurant, I say, *Oh, I love that place!* And of course it's more than having gained a steak; it's about enjoying a delicious meal where people cared about my experience. It all comes down to caring in the end.

The other day, we go to OfficeMax to buy a printer. It's a gigantic store. And they had one person working there. One person. That was it. Of course that poor salesperson working that store could not possibly meet the needs of every customer who walked in the door. It simply was not humanly possible. So this is a perfect example where the use of technology and the need for human interaction are clashing. Today, we have a-million-and-one choices of places where we can shop online. With just one click, I can get my desired merchandise delivered to my home. Why would I go to a brick and mortar store when I can go online and order it? Here is why: Because I want human interaction to walk me through my shopping experience. Isn't that what differentiates the brick and mortar store from the online purchase? It all comes down to providing a positive experience to your customers—and not just with any human, but a person who actually *cares*.

When shopping at Nordstrom or Bloomingdale's, the salesperson will often write you a note to thank you for your purchase. That's just good business.

In October of 2000, I bought Joyce a diamond ring from Costco. I lost the GIA certificate that provides all of the information about the diamond, including its size, quality, etc. I called Costco to get it, but because it had been more than seven years since the purchase, they had archived the records of our sale. As a result, they have put together a team of several people headed by a manager named Jennifer, in order to meet our request. Joyce and I are so impressed with their level of customer service. We received a call from Costco every day updating us on their progress. Costco really made us feel nurtured. At the end of nine days, they found all of the information and sent it to us! This tells me that Costco cares about meeting the needs of their customers. This is surprising for a large company. But again, this is good business. Here is what this experience has taught me: Costco is quality; the operative word is *caring*. In the end, it all comes down to only two factors: who cares and who doesn't. People want to be taken care of and they want to feel like they are important. That's it!

When Joyce and I bought our Tesla, I was not impressed with the man who sold it to us. When he closed the deal, he blurted his closing speech, a variation on the kind of closing speech that most salespeople across the country say to their customers. The thing that bugged me is that I could tell he was not connected to the words he was telling us. He was just doing a *job*. He was not providing us a service. I've sold insurance policies to clients a thousand times over, and when I did, I had closing words I'd say to them every time after the purchase was made, but it was never a spiel. And even though these words were more or less the same with each client, I can tell you that not once did I just blurt it out like it meant nothing. You know why? Because *each time* I said it, with *each* client, it was fresh for me. I made it fresh. I cared about that person and how I was changing their lives. It was not just a *job*. I was talking to them from a place of truth. *That* is the key to golden customer service: a relationship where you express to your customer that you *genuinely* care.

I went to Macy's the other day in the hopes of buying a pair of Levi's. I am not one of those self-shoppers. I appreciate a lot of help. I am just that kind of customer. The entire men's department was on one floor backed by two salespeople. Now that's not realistic. How can two people serve all of those customers in the way they need to be served? They can't. I found a pair of Levi's but I also wanted a few other things. It was a frustrating experience because I could not get the assistance I needed. So I left. How shortsighted are these large companies that allow customers to walk into a store and not provide them with proper assistance?

If you go to a restaurant and the food is good but the service is horrible, you want to know something? The food becomes horrible. That's what happens. If the whole experience is bad, your taste buds change.

The foundation of a client relationship is about showing that you genuinely care. Not just reading a speech or duping the customer into thinking that you care. Can robots care?

In the end, technology cannot replace the human experience, but it can certainly enhance it along the way. The thing is, I care about my clients. I care about being cared for and I care about caring.

You're Fortunate to Have Friends

The most lasting relationships are forged face to face, not Facebook to Facebook. I know that today people meet their future wives or husbands online and that these relationships can become wonderful, enduring bonds, yet in those cases it was the technology that initially brought the people together, but the forging and the bonding took place in person. Think back on how you forged your most profound relationships and your deepest friendships. Even if you met the love of your life online, you developed a meaningful and layered relationship through personal interaction. Relationships are based on shared experiences and memories. The best way to get to know someone is to experience in person how they react to the life challenges. Ultimately, people crave human contact.

Nothing can replace the complexity and depth of the human experience. If you don't agree with me on this, think back on how you forged your most profound friendships. These types of long-term friendships were often made over a period of years.

You're very fortunate in life if you have two friends. Really fortunate. But most of the people in your life are actually acquaintances. Before you tell me that I am wrong, ask yourself this: *What is a friend?* How would you define the word "friend"? I would say that a friend is a volunteer in your life who accepts you for what you are, as flawed as you may be, without judgment. That is a friend. And how much time in your life do you have to devote to your friend for him to be your friend? Your friend needs your attention. Your friend needs for you to listen and accept him as he is. Your friend requires your full acceptance.

Even if you missed making those lifelong friendships early on in your life, it's never too late to forge new friendships if you're older, but you will have to do so based on common interests. Something that is happening in both of your lives. The more momentous the shared experience, the stronger the bond. Maybe you both survived a cancer scare, or you've both adopted kids from overseas. Or you're going through a divorce. Whatever the case may be, you share a common history—this can be a good foundation for a future friendship.

Also, it is easier to become friends with people who are the same age as you because even if you don't have that long personal shared history behind decades of friendship with your friends from the past, you share the same cultural references. You grew up watching the same cartoons. You remember the same news events, the same cultural landmarks in your memories. Friendships are based on shared and common experiences.

So if you're a man in your 70s and you were raised in L.A. like me, you would remember *Road Side Beach*. You'd remember the Red Car. People nowadays don't know what the Red Car is. But all my friends remember it. This was a streetcar system we would ride all over the city. If somehow I made a new friend today who is the same age as me, we would share the same cultural and historical reference points from our years growing up separately. We would have all of that history in common. Just as your friends are the cornerstone of your social foundation, solid relationships are the cornerstone of any good business.

Mom-and-Pop Stores: A Vanishing America

Our country is changing. Here's what's not in America anymore: mom-and-pop stores. Stores like the ones I owned, stores where customers and owners know each other and form a bond.

I was speaking with someone on the phone the other day about Aspen, Colorado. They had not been there in over 20 years, and I said to them:

"You won't like it there anymore."

"What do you mean, I won't like Aspen?"

"Beauty is still there, but the soul of the town has left." I explained how the little mom-and-pop stores of 35 years ago have made way for places like Gucci, Cartier, and Versace. All those wonderful little stores where someone would walk in and they'd say, "Hey, John, how you doin'?" And he'd answer, "Great, Martha! How did your grandmother's surgery go?"

Those stores are gone. And do you know what those places provided that most new businesses today do not? Great personal service. That type of service is not a gimmick where the person calls the customer by their first name and blurts out memorized text. Great service is based on a relationship where the business cares, actually *cares* about the well-being of the customer. Think of a business that you love. Maybe it's your pharmacy. Why do you love your pharmacist? Because you trust them. Why do you trust them? Because you believe that they really do care about your well-being.

Be in the Relationship Business

I am in the relationship business. I can say to my long-term clients: So tell me, who do you still do business with now that you did 30 years ago?" And you know what they answer?

"That's you, Paul!" And they're right.

Most people in life want to connect. Most people want relationships. When we go out to the movies, we want to be able to turn to someone when it's over and say, "Hey, what did you think of the movie? Let's talk about it." What does this have to do with business? Everything! A business that succeeds is a business that makes its customers, clients, and patients feel secure. It is a business that connects with their customers by forging a relationship with them.

When I sell you insurance, you give me money and you get a piece of paper in return. You get this intangible thing that represents a guarantee that I will secure your tomorrow and most importantly, the tomorrow of your family members after you've gone. Could you make a better investment somewhere else? Maybe. Could you make a worse investment? Absolutely. Now that you've made the purchase, you're feeling good about your future security. And that's great. But what am I feeling? I feel overwhelmingly satisfied. Do you know why? Because I've provided you with a service that will enhance and change your life. No one else can give you what I've just provided for you.

When I first meet with my clients, I say to them, "Jane, you're 48 years old. Here is a canvas and a whole palette of paint—what would your life look like five years from now at 53?" And then Jane describes to me what she sees for herself in her life at 53. Then I say, "Let's use that palette to see what you can create for yourself at 58."

And I move Jane through the process of painting her future in incremental steps. What usually happens is that Jane will say, "I'm a bit worried about myself financially. It looks to me like I am not going to be safe. I don't just want to be okay; I want to be GREAT." So Jane makes a commitment to herself to become safer and more secure by engaging my services. It's a financial commitment for the next 20 years. How do I feel now? Do I say, "Whoopee, I made a commission"? Sure, I am happy I made a commission; that's how I make my living. But you know what? I feel great because I just did something wonderful for someone else. This scenario does not only pertain to just the insurance business. It's true of any business. Any good service will be a value added to the client's life.

If I'm in the market to buy a car and I buy a Ford from you, what have you done? You've sold me a reliable vehicle with a very good warranty. And you know I won't have to worry about this vehicle and that it is within my financial means. As a salesperson, how do you feel? You feel great. You're saying to yourself, *Wow, I gave him the right vehicle.* Do you feel good about this commission? Yes, of course. But you also feel good about the service you have provided me and the relationship you have built with me.

But here is the thing: When did you ever get a call from your car salesperson *after* they had already sold you the car? I am willing to bet that the answer to that question is *never.* That lack of follow-up with clients is something that has always baffled me about the automobile industry. The key to being a great salesperson is to not only develop, but to maintain a solid relationship with your customers.

Wouldn't it be nice if as the salesperson who sold me a car, you called me and said to me, "Hey, Paul, the car is a year old. How is it going?" You're not trying to bother me but to remind me that you're there for me if I need anything and most importantly, you're reminding me that you *care.* Call me up; send me a birthday card, a box of chocolates. Something. It's a connection. But guess whom I will call the next time I need to buy a car? I will call you! And maybe I'll buy two cars, one for me and one for my wife. Maintaining that connection is everything.

Let's say you want to buy a home in Palm Springs, CA, and you live in a small apartment that you're renting for $800 a month at the moment. You're looking for permanency. You want security. You want to live in a home. A home would be nice. Your rental apartment does not have adequate parking. You don't have a garage—you have a carport—and you certainly don't have a yard. I'm your real estate person and I walk you through a better situation and show you that as a first-time homeowner, you qualify for an FHA loan with only 3 percent down. I show you that with your current tax bracket of 35 percent, if you buy a home for $425,000, you will be paying $1,800 a month mortgage, $800 of which will be deductible. Your current rent is already $800 month, so now $1,000 a month after taxes to own your home doesn't look so bad. I show you a beautiful house on Bright Star Street, with a nice little fenced in yard for your dog and a sparkling swimming pool to cool off on those hot desert nights. Sure, the house needs a little bit of tender loving care but you happen to be handy. The house is listed at $465,000, but I get it for you for $425,000. You're ecstatic. I have given you independence, permanency, and pride. Where does the pride come from? *Knowing that this is what is mine.* I have provided you with a service that actually empowers. We're both delighted. You met with me and I have provided you with a home. How do you feel? Wonderful! I have given you the opportunity to be yourself. Priceless, isn't it? This is what it means to build a relationship in business.

The Powerful World of Referrals

The gentleman who ran my agency at Northwestern Mutual came to me one day and said, "There is this businessman interested in purchasing insurance, but I cannot give him the attention he deserves. Can you go out and see him?"

"I'd be glad to," I told him. I wasn't about to turn down an opportunity when I saw one. So I set up a meeting with this potential client. He ran a very successful business and he was a very serious, no-nonsense kind of man, who demanded high performance of the people around him. He knew exactly the kind of product he wanted. He was all business. This relationship put me on the map and represented a rocket ship to my success by opening enormous opportunities I did not know even existed. This moment was the single most important turning point of my career.

The prospective client related to me that his close friend was an insurance agent with another company. He wanted to compare the two companies. Northwestern Mutual and the company his friend represented. He requested a proposal for a certain amount of insurance from both companies. I recognized immediately that this was an excellent opportunity. I knew I had to be creative and come up with ideas that would differentiate me from my competition. This is one of the times in my life when I came up with an original idea. The meeting took place at the Beverly Hilton Hotel, and the prospective client had his two attorneys and five CPAs from his accounting firm present. I looked at these professionals sitting around the table and thought, *My gosh, how much does this meeting cost?* There was a lot at stake for me and I wanted to make sure that I was more than well prepared. In preparation for the meeting, I had put together a series of proposals and alternative solutions in a bound book and I made enough copies for each of the participants, including the competing agents.

Although he was an extremely successful man up until that point, my competition walks in with no written materials prepared. He seemed pretty shocked when I handed him my booklet with all of the proposals and all of the financial information on the company, including the comments from the financial rating companies such as S&P, Moody's, etc. My potential client's advisors loved how prepared I was because it made their life easier with everything they needed right at their fingertips.

The next day, I got a call telling me that the case was mine. Needless to say, I was over the top with joy. Of course the commission was quite large, but what made this transaction so meaningful and so impactful on my life is that the client referred me to his personal lawyer. And being that the client was so well respected, his lawyer in turn became a client. And that lawyer started referring me to his business associates and friends.

The magnitude of referrals in all businesses is an immensely powerful tool for success where each interaction is an opportunity to grow your business.

So I set up a time to meet with my client's referral, as I would usually do, and he wanted to go to Benihana, on Wilshire Boulevard, so I said okay. Let's go to Benihana, even though I usually go to a place where you can get a sandwich, and sit and talk. I learned something here. We sit down and the waitress comes over and asks, "Would you like something to drink?" My prospect orders a double scotch! Then, when it comes time to order something to eat, he says to the waitress, "I'll have the double steak and the double shrimp, and the double everything." When the check came, I had a triple bill. That was the last time I let that happen. Now, when I meet with potential and current clients and the waiter comes over and says, "Would you like something to drink?" I don't even let the person get a chance to answer. I just say, "Just soft drinks. This is a working meeting."

The Benihana guy was in the aluminum business and he became a client. The success of my business was built upon the power of referrals. Each of these clients was impressed with my service and my product and each referred me to their friends and business associates, who in turn referred me as well. I have always learned something from each of my clients. As long as you stay open to learning, you will continue to learn and grow in your business.

When I serve a client and serve them well, they produce 15 more clients like the tentacles of an octopus! This kind of victory with my first big break never would have happened without the enormous amount of preparation I did.

Give Me the Magic: 10-3-1

So a young man comes to see me, about 25 years ago. I am in the middle of my career where I have reached a certain level of success. This was a very nice young man. I knew his father very well.

"What do you do to be successful?" he asked me.

"I get on the phones and make appointments," I tell him.

"But what else do you do?"

"I work hard. I am either seeing clients or I am on the phone making appointments."

I explain to him how I work. I tell him about the power of the one-on-one meeting and the foundation of a successful business relying on relationships. When it's all over, he turns to me.

"You know, we're in your office and we're all alone, just the two of us. Come on, you can tell me; what do you *really* do? Give me the magic formula for your success."

"What?" I asked him confused.

"I want the magic. Give me the magic formula."

I looked at that kid square in the face and told him the only truth I knew.

"The magic of success is going to work every day. Doing what you're supposed to do. Doing the everyday grunt work. The magic is getting on the phone and making appointments. The magic formula is having to call ten potential clients, to meet three in person so that one of them becomes your client. *10-3-1.* That's the magic."

I am not sure if he believed me, but I was telling him the only truth I knew.

In business, as in personal relationships, the most difficult thing to do is to get the date or the appointment. Don't you find that to be true? If you meet someone you like, you want to get a date—that's the hardest part. The same is true in business. The most difficult thing to do is to get one appointment. One of the most difficult aspects of my business is getting on the phone and making appointments. It's tedious and hard. It's the least favorite part of my work because it's so difficult. You have to dial and dial to get to talk to somebody.

So, I scheduled time for calls in my weekly planner. I would block out Tuesday from 10–12 and Thursday from 1:30–4:30 just to make appointments. I never set up client appointments during that time because that was my time to be on the phone. So what I did to make it more palatable is that I treated that time as if it was a business appointment. It was very hard, but no matter what, I kept at it. I kept making appointments. Why? Because I know that all businesses thrive when you have enough new clients and existing clients coming through your door.

If you have only one appointment for the entire week, you're thinking, *Oh, my gosh*. And if the appointment is at 1:00, and you get a call at 12:30 from the potential client saying, "I can't make it," now it feels like the end of the world. But if you have 35 appointments, and ten of them cancel or postpone, it's not the end of the world. You move on. Life is not difficult. There are no miracles. There is no magic to any of it.

Buy What You Trust: Buy Cartier

Every great relationship is built on trust. Years ago, I wanted to buy my wife a diamond ring for no other reason than the fact that Joyce is an amazing wife. So, I asked around for reliable merchants. Of course, everybody knows somebody who knows somebody in the diamond business. "Oh you have to buy it from my guy. Danny the Diamond King—he is the best." So I call this guy up.

"My friend Jerry told me all about you." I tell him what I want and he says,

"Come down, and I'll show you some beautiful diamonds."

So I go down to the shop where he shows me a diamond with perfect clarity and grading from the Gemological Institute of America. The diamond was also within my budget. I wanted to look one more place before I made my final decision. So I said, "I will let you know tomorrow." The next day, I call him and say, "Danny the Diamond King, I am ready to get that diamond."

The problem with diamonds is it's a difficult product for a layperson to understand. What do most people know about the quality of diamonds? Personally, I knew nothing at all.

So, I go down to make my purchase and all of a sudden, the diamond I wanted is not there. There is another one in its place.

"Danny the Diamond King, what happened to yesterday's diamond?"

"This one is better!" he tells me.

Well, it wasn't better. It was a bait and switch routine. Preying upon my ignorance.

I had been looking now for four months, going to a lot of Danny the Diamond King-type stores. So, you know what I did? I went to Cartier. Why? Because I could trust them. I could guarantee that what I was buying was authentic. It is a Cartier stone with a Cartier design, Cartier everything. And if they tell you it's purple, it's purple. It's not dyed. You can trust them, and their diamonds are guaranteed.

The main job for these diamond guys is to lure you in with the desire to buy two and try to get you to buy four. There's no trust in that kind of relationship. In fact, there is no relationship at all. Trying to make a purchase from someone you cannot trust, and where there is no relationship whatsoever, is not a pleasant experience. When you sell blind products like diamonds, or insurance for that matter, you have to establish a solid relationship with a foundation of trust. People spend more time researching the purchase of a refrigerator than they do a life insurance policy. There are some very dubious products out there, and it is crucial to select someone you can trust. That's what I did. Cartier's reputation speaks for itself.

Ultimately, the foundation of any solid relationship is built on trust. If you're in the relationship business, if people trust you and feel that your product or service is great and that you have their best interest at heart, you will make a client for life. In general, why do clients leave a business? They leave because something happened that resulted in their trust being taken away from the relationship. If you want long-lasting client relationships, you will have to establish trust.

Over the years, a few clients have left me. Most recently, I just lost a 52-year-old client with two kids because he felt that at my age, I could no longer provide the type of ongoing service he wanted. You know what I did? I referred him to one of my younger, trusted colleagues. I told him, "Let me find someone for you whom you will be comfortable with for the long term." Not only that, but I offered to stay on and make myself available to my client and his new agent for the next year in case they needed me. Not only do I uphold the trust that has been granted me in a client relationship, but I also uphold my obligations in alignment with my ethics and my morals to the very end.

Every Life I Touch with My Business Is Instantly Improved

One of the fundamental reasons why I have thrived in my business is that my clients trust me. They feel that I have their best interest at heart. And I do. I know with absolute certainty that the service I provide and the work I perform improve every life I touch. Do you know what that feels like? It is invigorating; it is electrifying to know that the work I have done for over four decades has systematically improved the lives of my clients for several generations into the future.

When I talk to some younger agents and ask them, "Why are you trying to increase your client base?" Some of them have answered, "I just want to make a living." Wrong answer! This answer is wrong, not because it's not true but because by putting your motivation for money before the relationship with your client, you're creating an equation that is not sustainable in the long term. When you're thinking of fees instead of going after improving the lives of clients, you're setting yourself and your clients up for failure.

From the moment I made my first sale, I thought, *Oh my goodness, look what I did.* Right away, I knew this was the right occupation for me. That's why I took to it like a duck takes to water. I said to myself, *If this person dies, I've taken care of their family. Assuming they live with a life expectancy beyond retirement, look at the cash that I'll provide for them to supplement their income.* What a feeling! It is this realization of the positive impact my work has had on the lives of my clients that has built my self-esteem and level of confidence into the rock-solid foundation of my business.

Life Lesson Moment

Most people have an untapped potential in their existing network of people. Dear reader, take a moment right now to make a list of all of the people in your current network of friends, family, and community members who could become potential clients for your business. Don't do what most people do and allow your existing network to be untapped. Don't be afraid to dig deeply into all of the people you know and with whom you've had contact along the way. Start with your immediate network of friends and family and move on out into the fringes of friends of friends, their coworkers and colleagues or clients. Of course, you may not readily know who your people know but you can certainly identify a core group of people with whom you already have a solid relationship that you can ask about possible referred leads. You will be amazed by the power of your untapped network.

I'll never forget when my clothing store business ended, I made a list of the 125 names from my Rolodex (the equivalent of a digital contact list today) and I acquired three clients. That was the point at which I moved from my untapped network to developing possible referred leads. The power of developing your network is the gold mine of your business today.

How to Enhance Your Business Using Technology

Technology is only as effective as the person who uses it. Relationships are built in person, but technology is a powerful way to maintain, enhance, and propel your client relationships to the next level. The key to using technology successfully in business is to find the perfect balance between face-to-face communication and creative technology solutions that enhance the contact you've already established in person.

Action Steps

Don't allow technology to be your primary communication tool. Nothing can replace the effectiveness of a face-to-face encounter or a physical letter, especially in the early phases of your client relationship. However, used correctly, technology can enhance and even strengthen a relationship already established face to face. Make sure you combine various technology solutions such as email, texting, e-blasts, Skyping, etc.... and stay in close contact with your clients. Decide upfront how you will combine technology and face time and stick to your plan. As you watch your client relationships blossom, adjust your plan accordingly.

Pick up the phone. Make sure you regularly speak to your clients. Schedule actual phone conversations with them to catch up and find out how they are doing. Remember that the quality of the connection established in person cannot be replaced by communicating only by text or email. Keep that human connection alive!

Personalize your technology communication. Whenever you send out information to your clients, personalize it. Sometimes e-blasts make sense, but whenever possible, include a small personal note at the top that lets the client see they matter to you.

Pay attention to how the client communicates. If a client seems to prefer phone, text, or in-person communication, make a note of it and make sure you honor their preferred style while maintaining your own dedication to person-to-person contact. Find a happy balance between the client's style, yours, and the demands of the day.

Match the medium to the message. Make sure you use the right medium for the right message. If you want to distinguish yourself and have something very important to say, write a letter! If you are trying to book an appointment with a busy person or figure out something complex, pick up the phone. It will make it easier on everyone. If you only want confirmation of a small piece of information and you've recently spoken with a client, feel free to use email. Use your instinct to maintain a balance between these various modes of communication.

Make a splash on social media. Your online presence must be well planned and executed. Don't slap your logo on Facebook or LinkedIn and call it a day. Make sure your posts meaningfully connect back to your brand and mission. Strive to provide content, so followers get daily value from this connection. Remember that your competition is taking advantage of these platforms and so should you. One caveat: Don't bombard your followers with inane content. This negates your credibility. Post less, and make sure your content is good.

Keep your website young and agile. Successful companies have streamlined, up-to-date websites. If it's been a while since you've changed your design, your website is long overdue for a tune-up and a facelift! Move with the times by updating to modern fonts, colors, and layouts. Is your website in alignment with your business image and your mission? Make sure your website is as professional and sleek as your own personal appearance when meeting a client for the first time. Your online presence should be a perfect reflection of the professional image you want to project at all times.

Use email to send links to articles you think your client might enjoy. In the philosophy of priming human contact and solidifying your personal connection to your clients, send them little links and articles you know they will enjoy. This gesture shows that you are thinking about them, that you know where their interests lie and that you care. But do keep these communications in balance. Bombarding clients with superficial links and articles may in fact weaken the value of your contact with them and ultimately undermine your relationship.

Allow clients to login and access their information. Whenever possible, empower clients by putting information at their fingertips. Are there ways that you can give your clients access to a login or online information? This not only saves time for your clients when they need to get a small piece of information, but it empowers them along the way.

Skype your meetings when you (or they) are traveling. Though it shouldn't completely replace in-person interactions, Skyping is a great way to keep in touch virtually with customers. This is true of contact with already-established client relationships. Try to avoid relying on Skype with clients you barely know. Remember that your relationship foundation should be established face to face, as much as possible. Which are your clients that would most benefit from an upcoming Skype call? Schedule it today.

Send e-newsletters to all your clients. Communicating via e-newsletter is just another way to engage with clients and stay on their minds. Create engaging content that connects with the various lines of services you are currently offering and craft interesting articles for your clients around related topics. Having a dynamic newsletter is also a great way to advertise upcoming events or new services that you provide.

PART FOUR

Achieving Confidence and Self-Esteem

The nature of self-confidence is elusive. When you're young, you have the exuberance of youth pushing you forward. Your lack of experience is often matched by an over-inflated level of confidence that is not fueled by actual achievement or skill but simply by a drive for life. This is a time when you have passion and you think you can do anything, the way I did when I started my clothing store business. In other words, you don't know any better.

CHAPTER TWELVE

The Elusive Nature of Self-Confidence

"*M*y complete ignorance about my own limitations looked like confidence. My belief that I could do these things contrary to my ability was half the battle; the other half was very hard work.*"*
—*Natalie Portman*

Everyone Is Insecure

Now that you've mastered your ability to make ends meet above the threshold of survival and have created a secure environment for yourself, you've also begun to find ways to develop a sense of love and belonging in the world. But without self-confidence, how can you build that empire you've always dreamt of building? How can you master the dream of self-actualization where waking up every morning is a delight and not an opening of the eyes followed by the weight of the world on your shoulders? Developing a solid sense of self, built on the foundation of strong self-esteem and confidence is a crucial aspect of your quest for overall success.

The famous actress Natalie Portman enrolled at Harvard University when she was 18 years old. By then, she had already been acting for seven years and she had achieved a respectable level of fame around the country and the world. In spite of these undeniable levels of achievement, she later admitted that on the first day of classes she was still very much insecure about whether or not she was smart enough to grace the halls of Harvard University. In 2015, Portman gave the commencement speech to the Harvard graduating class. In her opening lines she said, "Twelve years after graduating, I am still insecure about my own worthiness." Imagine that—a young woman who has been in 35 films, has won an Oscar, and is now directing her own films in addition to graduating from one of the most prestigious universities in the world—is still unsure about whether or not she is worthy. Everyone has insecurities, regardless of the levels of achievement and prestige obtained.

The nature of self-confidence is elusive. When you're young, you have the exuberance of youth pushing you forward. Your lack of experience is often matched by an over-inflated level of confidence that is not fueled by actual achievement or skill but simply by a drive for life. This is a time when you have passion and you think you can do anything, the way I did when I started my clothing store business. In other words, you don't know any better.

Go Beyond Your Horizons

A few years into owning my stores and ironically shortly before going bankrupt, I thought I was a big shot when in fact I was not. I thought I knew what I was doing and I felt I was the center of the universe, but in fact, I was none of those things. Of course, you know the end of that chapter in my life: I lost everything and had to start over at 36. I had hit rock bottom and I had nowhere to go but up—this included my level of confidence plummeting down to zero, along with my bank balance. Insecurity can be a great fuel for moving forward. In her commencement speech, Portman said, "The very experience that had made me feel insecure made me take risks." Whether you're hitting rock bottom or you're in the wonderful throes of the distorted self-importance of your youth, you should go beyond your horizons, put yourself in a situation you've never tried before, and go after a goal.

When Portman discusses making the transition from acting to directing, she admits that, like anyone trying something new for the very first time, she faced the limitations of her own experiences. She says, "My complete ignorance about my own limitations looked like confidence. My belief that I could do these things contrary to my ability was half the battle; the other half was very hard work." I am a proponent of consistent and diligent work. I don't necessarily like the phrase "hard work." Instead, I believe in "smart work." But the central point here is this: Your own self-perception, as well as the perception of others in the form of a vote of confidence, can be a very powerful validating tool that can propel you towards new horizons.

Years ago in my business, we used to be able to obtain clients for two parallel policies, one paid upfront and the second one non-prepaid. We are not allowed to do this anymore because of compliance, but the story I am about to tell you will show just how powerful validating someone's potential can be to move them into a new stratosphere of success.

I'd sit with my client and we'd go through the whole fact-finding process, where I'd gather all of the necessary information about them ranging from income to long-term financial goals. I would look the person in the eye, I would listen to them carefully, listen to their dreams and what they wanted to accomplish and discuss how they were going to achieve it. Let's say my client wanted a $2 million policy. I would give them two applications. I would collect the money for the first policy and then would submit the second one as non-prepaid. The company would issue the policies. And then I would say to my client, "Here's your $2 million policy. You know, the company looked at your financial situation, and it looks like your financial future is very bright. We looked at the projections for your financial performance over the next few years, and your potential looks to be almost unlimited. The company really feels that you're just at the beginning and that you're going to have a breakthrough at any point and that you're going to be cascading with money and success. Your whole life is going to open up globally. And for that reason, we are issuing you an additional $3 million of insurance for a total of $5 million because we feel that this is what you deserve and need." My client would listen to me attentively and think about what I was saying. Because I want him to expand his horizon, I invite him to invest in his full potential. Not just the level of achievement that he had already reached or what we could see emerging on the horizon of his life but the potential of greatness he could *actually* achieve. I believed every word I said to my client. I believed it because it was all true. He did in fact have this incredible potential to reach a level of greatness.

And with this approach, I had invited my client to look beyond his horizon, to look far into the distance at the majestic skyline opening right in front of him. And guess what happened every single time I did that with a client? They rose to the occasion and manifested their full potential, took their life to the next level of success, and took that second policy, every single time. It is incredible to look back now and see how impactful and effective validating someone else's potential could be on their life. This external vote of confidence propelled my clients forward every single time. It leads them to think, *Wow, this man has given me his vote of confidence and propelled my career to the next level.*

Realize Your Potential

Many people don't realize their potential. There are times when we all need someone to help us see beyond ourselves. You need to believe what somebody says about you, if it's a positive. Many people—like Natalie Portman the day she began classes at Harvard—have this aura of confidence, but inside, that's not how they feel. Inside they are thinking, *Am I really worthy of being in this situation of possible success?*

I was a paperboy from Culver City. I was the assembly line kid at Carnation, right? And at some point in my young life, I had to make a decision to start believing that I could do more than making pineapple sherbet. At some point, I had to take the golden ring from the merry-go-round. That is true for anyone who dreams of realizing some level of triumph.

At some point in your life, you need to accept that you can achieve your goals, in spite of whatever collateral baggage you may have. Let's face it, I did not have the rosiest childhood in the world, and because of my background, I had to make internal changes.

It has been my experience that many people have challenged childhoods. If you dig below the surface, some may have had parental problems. There are no perfect parents. Parents do the best they can. There are adults walking around in our world today that have placed blame on their parents for their own shortcomings.

Look at Demaryius Thomas of the Denver Broncos, for example. Both his mother and grandmother were arrested and convicted for drug dealing, leaving Demaryius to have to decide whether he would get stuck in this tragic beginning or move forward and make something of his life. Of course, he chose the latter.

The point of this story is that the past is the past. This is the case for your life as well. Now is the time to accept what has happened, live in the present, look forward to the future, and move on. Make your statement in life, now.

Finding Your Sense of Self

As you move through your own experiences, you will realize that there is always someone out there who can do it better, cheaper, faster than you can. There is always somebody who has more. More of what? Who knows and who cares? Whatever insecurities you might be carrying around, harness them in your favor. Being insecure is not a bad thing. It can actually be an asset. Self-esteem? What is self-esteem? I don't even know what it means. Do I feel good about myself? I feel a variety of things about myself. I feel that I have achieved more than I ever thought I would. Do I have self–esteem? Not when I stand next to that golfer who hits the ball 250 yards—and it's a woman.

So self-esteem, all these catchphrases and words are just words that give you an excuse to not do something. *Oh, poor me*—and all that self-pitying that some people do because they have faced challenges in their lives gives them an excuse not to go for it and make something out of their lives. So, if you want to move forward, you have to define who you really are and not let outside influences give you excuses to become paralyzed. The true measure of success perhaps is that moment when you finally find the ability to develop your own sense of self.

Are You a One-Note Charlie?

One afternoon, we were driving from L.A. to our home in Palm Springs while listening to Kiss radio. They were playing all of the one-hit wonders. The two-and-a-half-hour drive allowed us to hear quite a few songs that had become massive hits but had never been followed by another success. Turns out, this "one-hit wonder" phenomenon is very common. It made me realize that I don't want to be a one-hit wonder. Do you?

After I had the taste of my first big success three years into my career in the insurance business, I was plagued with the fear of having become a one-hit wonder. Even when you reach your first level of success, you are vulnerable to insecurities. *Oh my gosh, am I a one-note Charlie? Can I ever do it again?* I had to ask myself, *What was the formula that allowed me to have this first success? I want to do it again.* If somehow you gain access to the kingdom like I had at that point in my career, you have to realize that it is a very big castle. How will you get around? What will you do in there? Just because somebody has referred you or you get that extra client or whatever it happens to be, that's just the beginning. Now is NOT the time to rest on your laurels. You have to earn it and make the most of it so that you don't become that one-note Charlie.

Three years into my career, I was finally starting to see signs of true success; this was a visceral feeling that I loved and I wanted to experience again. It's an amazing feeling to be recognized. Unlike these earlier moments when I was struggling to find myself, I wanted to continue that success over and over again. I was no longer in the exuberance of my youth nor in the panic of my post-bankruptcy scramble. Instead, I simply wanted to know the answer to the terrifying question: *Can I do it again?* Waiting for the answer to that question to make itself known can make for a very long and terrifying waiting period.

For the longest time, I thought that I was a flash in the pan. I took my Chevy to the levy but the levy was dry. These are the lyrics from Don McLean's song "American Pic" that hit the number-one charts in 1972, but also represents the only great hit of his life. Sure, he went on to write and release many other songs after that, but he never, ever again reached that level of acclaim. This was my greatest fear after that first big break. Just because you have one big success does not mean you can say, *I made it.* Now you have to repeat it and repeat it. You don't have that comfort of complacency. What you have is the comfort of saying: *I have to keep working hard to do it again.*

Luckily, I kept doing it year after year. Fear was a motivator that never really went away. And then one day it dawned on me: *Oh my gosh, I've been doing this for 42 years.* That's a long note. I think I've written a symphony. Good thing I am not a tuba player holding this note; otherwise, I'd be in deep trouble.

In the end, succeeding requires some kind of suspension of disbelief that you can transform yourself into the hero of your own story. Believing that you can beat the odds requires an unrelenting desire to apply yourself and achieve your own measure of success. And most of all, success requires you to have the courage to push your fear away and not let it rule your decisions and your life. If you think about the long list of obstacles you may or may not face along the way, you will become paralyzed with fear. The only thing to remember is this: How many push-ups can I do today? How many push-ups do I want to be able to do tomorrow? What do I need to do today to get there?

Develop Your Own Measure of Success

Natalie Portman gives those young Harvard graduates wonderful advice when she says, "Achievement is wonderful when you know why you're doing it, and when you don't, it can be a terrible thing." This brings us to the notion of the measure of success. Are you measuring your success by the standards and opinions of others, by the typical and often wonderful trappings of society including fame, power, and wealth? Or are you gauging your progress by your own measure of how much you are enjoying something, how close the work keeps you to who you are, and what difference you are making in the world, if any? By now you should know this about me: I love the wonderful trappings of my own success. I love my homes and flying first class and being able to acquire an art collection over the years. But most of all, I love the fact that we've been able to make impactful charitable contributions. But is this what measures my success?

When Portman did her first film, *Léon: The Professional*, it tanked so terribly that the press wrote, "Portman poses better than she acts." That early failure was a defining moment for Portman. She could have decided that she was not really cut out for acting after all and quit her career, but instead she got back up and turned this challenge into an opportunity for growth. What can only be seen as a failure, on the outside, was in all actuality a success of sorts for Portman. After all, aren't we all striving to develop a clear sense of self, a sense that we know exactly what we truly love to do and how to go about doing it? This failure became the definitive moment when she decided to do only work that she feels passionate about. She was only 14 years old.

Life Lesson Moment

The perception of others in your claim for success can be a double-edged sword. If someone believes in you, the way I believed in some of my clients, it can help propel you to the next level of achievement and success in your life. But if the perception is negative, it can also paralyze you. The key is to ignore the naysayers and use adversity to your advantage. Remember when I lost everything and I had to start over at age 36? What if I had stopped there and never stood back up again? Many people hit a wall and never get back up. The key to continuously moving through challenges and striving for success time and time again is to find the excitement in life in learning new things. And in doing so, you enjoy your life regardless of whether or not the world is applauding or booing you.

You must hang in there for the long haul, because no matter what you do, and no matter what industry you're in, you will run into a wall of some kind at some point of the ride. These walls can and will come in many forms. For some of you, it will mean getting laid off or even fired. For others, your business will become obsolete and you will have to find a way to reinvent yourself and go after a new market. No matter what form your challenge takes, remember that facing these trials is what gives life great beauty and its excitement. No matter what happens, you have to constantly be dynamic and adapt. You may not like it at that time. But it doesn't make any difference, because any time you overcome one of these speed bumps, or walls, or it's a 10,000-foot crevasse that you just fell into, every time you overcome one of those, you become bigger, and stronger, and richer, and your self-confidence soars.

Take a moment to write down the names of the nay-sayers in your life. Are there people in your environment who are telling you directly or indirectly that you cannot succeed in achieving your goal? Now think about the ways in which you can silence those naysayers. Sometimes, it might be as simple and direct as removing those people from your life. But this may not always be possible. Instead, how can you ignore those naysayers by stripping them of the power you've granted them? Now that you've identified the naysayers in your life, take a moment to write down the champions in your life. Who are they? Are you nurturing those relationships with your champions as much as you can? If not, what can you do today to further develop and grow those connections?

How to Apply the Push-Up Principle to Your Goals

The push-up principle is one of the most powerful methods of transforming your life and your business by starting out at whatever starting point you are at today and moving on up. Victories are achieved incrementally through daily perseverance. Regardless of your current level of expertise or skill, you can start making strides towards improving your level of performance today. Every step you reach along the way is a stepping stone for your continued development to the next level.

Action Steps

Assess your starting point. Even if you're starting out "small" such as going into business for yourself, going back to school, or starting over in life, you can achieve a life of abundance using the push-up principle. Take an honest look in the mirror and assess where you are now. Define concretely what you would like to achieve and move incrementally from your starting point forward. You can only do five push-ups? No problem! Do six for a few days and keep increasing. Don't get discouraged by your current position in life—you are about to change everything, starting now.

Choose your finish line. Before you can begin a long legacy of achievement, you have to figure out where you want to go. So write down the concrete goals you intend to achieve. Some examples might be: I want to run a successful consulting firm and hire ten new employees within two years. I want to increase my salary by $100K each year for the next five years. I want to make enough money to have the option to retire. Remember, once you reach those goals, you can set bigger goals and use the push-up principle to achieve them.

Commit to a personal growth mindset. You can achieve your own success by making ongoing progress in whatever goal you have set. Keep in mind that growth can sometimes be uncomfortable, but if you commit to growing a little bit every day, over time your life will change in remarkable ways. Make a plan to commit to working toward the prize on a daily basis. Pick one goal you would like to achieve this week and put the push-up principle to work. Increase your progress on a regular basis and watch yourself get to the finish line before you know it.

Set small reasonable goals and immediately work to achieve them. The push-up principle allows you to set small, achievable goals and methodically achieve them. This may seem overwhelming at first, especially if you don't have a proven record of success behind you, but have faith. Small goals are easy to cross off and they give you confidence that yes, you are in control and can make things happen in your life! Practice them daily, and they will get easier as you grow more comfortable with the concept.

Build on your momentum. Once you've gotten used to setting reasonable goals and achieving them, keep going and expand your efforts. At this point, you've proven to yourself that you can make things happen, so keep setting your sights just outside of what you believe you can achieve, and keep outperforming yourself. What are the next set of goals you'd like to achieve and put through the push-up principle?

Keep pushing when you want to quit. When you are making this level of progress, you may encounter moments of struggle or conflict. During these moments of adversity, put your head down and keep working, instead of stalling out. You'll get through the rough patches and be able to continue on your upward climb. Take a breather and look back at your successes so far using the push-up principle and relish in the feeling that you're already a winner with everything you've accomplished so far. Now get back to the grindstone and keep forging ahead to the next level of achievement.

Apply the push-up principle to all areas of your life. This principle isn't just for your work life. It can help you improve your diet, fitness level, your spiritual life, your relationship, family relationships, and anything else you set out to accomplish. Try using this principle to add more nutritious foods to your diet, to add an extra mile to your workout, or to increase the time you spend in meditation or prayer. With small amounts of effort, you can enrich countless aspects of your daily life, bringing you greater joy and satisfaction.

Turn away from complacency. When you start experiencing success such as making more money, surpassing your sales goals, or gathering more clients, it might be tempting to feel satisfied and slow down. Push past this impulse! Complacency always stalls your progress. At the first sign of complacency, take a moment to revisit your goals and re-motivate yourself to stay on course with the set of goals you have decided to achieve.

Make a plan for when you hit a wall. Don't be surprised if all this forward motion causes you to reach a point of exhaustion. It happens, but it's always temporary—or at least it should be! Have a game plan prepared for those moments you feel burned out. Re-read this book, call a friend who has agreed to keep you accountable, or get centered by going to the gym, meditating, or hiking. Read something inspirational. Just do something that will help get you back on track.

CHAPTER THIRTEEN

Work Smarter, Not Harder

A wonderful man in our agency writes lots of policies and makes a modest living doing it. The reason he does not make great money is because he thinks four inches rather than a foot. He thinks: Well, this person only needs $100,000 of insurance. One day I finally said to him, "Everybody needs a minimum of a million." This poor guy is pedaling really hard. He has no gears. He has that old Schwinn bike; it's not even a 3-speed. Sometimes, it's not a matter of having to pedal harder, but having to get more gears.

Stop, Look, and Listen

One of the greatest principles I have put to work in my own business is my ability to stop, look, and listen and build upon the existing assets in my life. So many people are off pedaling furiously in their business to make it happen, but at the end of each day, they go to sleep exhausted without being one step farther than they were the day before. This prolonged effort with standstill results can be taxing on your level of self-confidence, and it might be a good indicator that you could benefit from identifying your assets and building upon them. How do you do that? Stop, look, and listen.

One of my favorite movies is *Casablanca*. I must have watched it a dozen times. Who doesn't love Humphrey Bogart and the gorgeous Ingrid Bergman? How gorgeous and classy was she? Pure beauty.

One day my friend Jim and his wife, Bunny—who has since passed away from pancreatic cancer—invite Joyce and me to come for a Labor Day shindig at their house and watch *Casablanca* on their brand-new plasma TV. The ladies are all downstairs playing Bridge while the guys and I sit down in front of a monster screen. The movie opens in a bazar in Casablanca with a crowd of people craning their necks in order to see a plane flying overhead. This was an unusual enough occurrence to be the cause for commotion. As the plane flies, the camera pans to the first person, and then the second, and the third, when suddenly my heart lurches in my chest. I can't believe my eyes.

"Jim, stop! Go back, rewind!" I yell.

He rewinds.

"Stop!" I yell again. I couldn't believe it. There was my father in the frame! He was 32 years old—a handsome fellow with full head of hair. How shocking to see my own father working as an extra in my favorite film! I must have watched it a dozen times but had never noticed him before.

This anecdote has made me realize just how easy it is for all of us to miss what is right in front of our eyes. Of course, this was an old movie, and the frames were poor quality (before digitization) and yes, I'd watched it all of those times on a tiny black and white TV instead of my friend's large home screen. But regardless of these points, the fact remains that I had missed something I'd *seen* a dozen times. This experience made me ask myself: *What else have I missed that has been right in front of my face?* How oblivious are we sometimes that we miss the essentials, right in front of us?

Allow me to give you some advice, dear reader: *Stop, look,* and *listen*. Pause a moment and take a snapshot of your own life. Ask yourself if you're fulfilled with your current professional situation, and if not, establish what might be missing. What assets do you already have that have not yet been developed? In other words, assess whether or not you are working efficiently. I have witnessed individuals squandering their most important asset: time. Here they are, working and earning a living, but they have no money. Some of them might see that 60-year-old coworker and secretly scorn them for working at the same place so late in life and having nothing to show for it. They might be thinking, *That's not going to be me.* If any of this reflects your experience and thoughts, I would ask you this very important question: What steps are you taking today to ensure that you will not be in a dead-end job at age 60? Are you giving yourself an opportunity to build success and monetary growth for your future?

Whenever one examines the small businesses that go under, they all seem to share one thing in common: They are undercapitalized and run inefficiently. When I owned my four clothing stores, I was a perfect example of the inefficient small business owner. My main problem came in the form of ego and the fact that I wanted to impress the vendors with whom I was doing business. If I needed four of something, I would buy ten so they would think more of me. I did not stop, look, and listen. In fact, I didn't mind my stores, and it cost me everything.

Stop, look, and listen. This is a golden rule. If you're in the lightbulb business and you're not making LED lights, your business is at risk. The world is in constant flux. You have to remain flexible. Making decisions to better your life and expand your opportunities is not rocket science. You don't have to be Albert Einstein to realize that the book publishing business is changing, dramatically. Once upon a time, it used to require a hundred lawyers to carry out a merger but with today's technology and efficiency, it might take only three or four. There are revolutions going on in every industry. I now drive a Tesla that is run by batteries instead of a conventional fossil-fuel engine. While you take your car to a gas station and later get an oil change and a tune-up, I'm getting a software upgrade on my car as my Tesla sits in my garage. If you want to be successful in your industry, you're going to have to remain relevant. This means staying informed, remaining in the know of all of the changes and opportunities lurking right around the corner. All of this is really a matter of survival. Isn't it?

Stop what you're doing, look around, listen to your life, and say, *Is this what I want?* And if the answer to that question is "no," then I would suggest you make a change today. Not tomorrow or next week. Today. Don't miss what is right in the frame of your own movie.

Don't Pedal Harder. Get More Gears!

We all know one thing for sure: None of us is getting out of this alive. The biggest certainty in life is its very end. So how are you going to ride your bike all the way through? As I get older, I've noticed that efficiency is more important than ever before. Here I am at 78 years of age, and just like that poor salesman selling only $100,000 policies, I now need more gears because I can't pedal that hard anymore. Certainly this is true in the literal sense on my afternoon cycling trips around Cordillera in Colorado where I live, but it is also the case metaphorically speaking. In my own business, getting more gears means gaining access to more knowledge about my industry and about new products and services that will affect how I work. Once I gain this additional information, the pedaling gets easier.

I learned years ago that the more I know, the more options I gain, and therefore the more choices I have. At some point in your life, and hopefully sooner than later, the moment will come for you to trade in that 3-speed bicycle for a 21-speed bike. That will be the very moment when you begin working smarter rather than harder. As you develop efficiency in the way you conduct your business, you will increase your confidence, which in turn will free up more energy for you to focus on the most important phase of your success: achieving self-actualization.

Define Your Market; Go After It

So, you don't have to go out and reinvent the wheel in order to conduct a successful business. No, in fact, the only thing you have to reinvent is the focus of your market. One of the key aspects of working smarter is to identify and get into that marketplace.

Whether you're a doctor or a lawyer, you will have to define the direction in which you would like to go and make changes in your life in order to reach it. If you look at the medical profession nowadays, everyone is a specialist. General practitioners are diminishing. You can be a doctor without borders, or you could be a plastic surgeon in Beverly Hills. Define your market and go after it. It is that simple.

The key to finding that new marketplace lies in your ability to upgrade your clientele. Remember when I realized that I had to go from doctors to business managers as my primary target client? This was a turning point in my career. Because there are more business opportunities on the Westside of Los Angeles, I moved my office to that area 25 years ago.

As a businessman, I have multiple goals. My primary goal is that you know, as my client, that the product that I have provided for you is the finest product in the country today. You know that my office will provide to you the best service and care for you and your family. With those two elements, it is inevitable for you to have financial success as a result. I am here to tell you that when you work smarter, and therefore more efficiently, one of the byproducts of this change is often making more money. For example, say you're in the women's clothing business and you need to expand your clientele to include men. You will have broadened your scope and increased your revenue. But perhaps you are content where you are. You're thinking: *Gosh, I make $150,000 a year and I'm pretty happy. I am never going to live in an $8 million home, but I feel pretty good.* Then you're successful. Living in Beverly Hills is not everyone's dream. Remember the push-up principle, where the definition of being number one is to surpass your own previous capabilities? If you used to make $75,000 and now you're actually making twice as much, then you're your very own number one. How good is that? Here you are, having changed a few things in your business in order to run more efficiently, and without any additional effort, you've now doubled your income.

Life Is Deep—Is It?

I once heard a tale about a man who climbed to the top of the Himalaya Mountains in order to hear the wisdom of a famous yogi of the world. The climber trained and prepared for weeks and months in order to make this meeting possible. He would wake at dawn and begin to climb, carrying his heavy gear. He faced the treacherous heat at midday and the debilitating cold at nightfall. The climb took many days, pushing him to the edge of his own physical limitations. Finally, upon reaching the top of the mountain and seeing the yogi sitting there, eyes closed, legs crossed, in that stereotypical yogi pose, the climber says to the yogi, "Life is deep." To which the yogi replies, "Is it?"

Life is not that deep; it's not that complicated. Define what you want to accomplish and go after it. And if you want to catch a glimpse of the way your life will unfold tomorrow, simply notice the decisions you are making in your life today. After all, your future is nothing but a reflection of the decisions you are making now. Deep? I don't think so.

Think a Foot Rather Than an Inch

If you're operating in a marketplace that does not offer you opportunities for economic growth, are you limiting your scope or could you possibly envision yourself in a broader reach? The first step to building your success is to identify your target market. One of the difficulties facing many professionals is finding how to get to that audience.

If you decide that you want to start going after a more affluent market, you may come to realize that you're not working with the same clientele anymore. Maybe you're eyeing the Benz salesperson wearing that gorgeous suit at work while you're buying all of your clothes at Target. Nothing wrong with that, but if you want to make more money, then you're going to have to upgrade your clientele. How are you going to go about doing that? If you're in the insurance business and you're selling to middle-management workers at General Motors and Ford, how are you going to go about selling to executives instead? What steps are you going to take to get there?

Here's a tip: Everybody knows somebody who is operating in a loftier economic scale. Most people have doctors, lawyers, and accountants. Traditionally these people live in a higher bracket than most.

Remember the *Life Lesson Moment* exercise at the end of Chapter 11 where you identified your available network of people? Here is the time to build upon that exercise and actively work towards obtaining referred leads. Now is the time for you to work with people you already know and have them refer you to the professionals in their life. What does that mean? It's simple: Approach people in your current network and reach out to the doctors and lawyers of your existing clients and their current network. This tactic can facilitate your ability to make a quantum social leap into the higher echelons of the networks where you've already been operating.

I've always been taught there is only one captain of a ship, one engineer of a train. These individuals are mere mortals, yet they carry the weight of tremendous responsibility on their shoulders. This is true of your life as well. If you muster the ability to command a great presence in the room while meeting with your clients, they will remember that you have the knowledge and the ability to successfully guide them through their challenges. Your client is putting their faith in your ability to make the changes necessary for them to have the life they would like to lead.

Once you have determined that you're the captain of your ship, what you're doing now is smarter, not harder. You're working with the confidence that you are the one in the room who has the knowledge. Your client is putting their faith in you to guide them to a correct decision. It's not always the person who works the hardest who is the most successful. Instead, it is the person who has the commanding experience, knows their product, and knows their marketplace. That is the individual who in the end makes the most money and becomes financially successful.

Now, I want to talk about the phenomenon of the Girl Scouts selling cookies. In just seven weeks, more than 175 million boxes of cookies are sold, grossing between $700 and $800 million in sales each year. And like every business, there is a number one salesperson for that industry. The greatest Girl Scout cookies salesperson ever was a 13-year-old girl from Fairfax, Virginia, named Elizabeth Brinton. In her entire career as a Girl Scout selling cookies, which spanned the entire 1980s, Elizabeth sold more than 100,000 boxes of Girl Scout cookies. When asked how she did it, Elizabeth distilled her success into four basic principles:

1. Set high goals.
2. Sell yourself and your products.
3. Know your territory and customers.
4. Accept the fact that some people will say no.

Elizabeth would often say to her potential clients, "Why don't you buy a whole case? You can always freeze them." Smart girl. Why sell one box of cookies when you can sell an entire case, right?

Before long, that little girl was giving speeches to grown men about how to succeed in business. Today, Elizabeth Brinton is a corporate strategist at PG&E in San Francisco. She thought a *foot* rather than an *inch*. Sometimes, a word makes a world of difference.

If you're in the first years of your new business, know that you're going to have to weather the storm. The reality is that when you start a new business, it takes an average of three years for your business to get off the ground. During that time, you will be pedaling like crazy. There is no way around that. And many of those times you will be pedaling uphill. Just remember that one of the essential lessons of working smarter and not harder is about going after the right target audience with the clients who can afford to pay your fees. Stay focused, work hard, and weather those three years with your clear plan of action, and you will come out on the other side with a solid foundation for the years ahead.

Life Lesson Moment

Dear reader, now that we've clearly established that it is wise to work smarter rather than harder, I would like to offer you a little exercise and a tip to accomplish just that. Remember when I realized that my father was in the frame of the *Casablanca* movie I had seen a hundred times? We often miss what is right in front of our eyes. The best thing you can do for yourself is to become better acquainted with your existing assets so that you can go on to develop what I call "stackable goals." There is a theme that keeps coming up over and over again in my life and therefore in this book; the theme is this: *We often don't make the most of what we already have.* This is true of maximizing the power of your existing social business networks, but also in realizing the power of your own skills. This concept of using your existing assets and wisdom in order to maximize your success is certainly not a new concept. It is also used in arenas like sports medicine, where physical therapists work closely with injured athletes, using their bodies' existing strength and neurological wisdom in order to heal themselves. You can apply this concept to every aspect of your life. I guarantee that if you take your existing assets and maximize upon them, you will revolutionize your own life and business in the process.

Take a moment to write down some of the things you've managed to accomplish in your life so far. These achievements can be things like writing a book, raising my son, and launching my new business. Now write down the skills that you currently possess and used in order to accomplish these tasks. This little exercise will urge you to acknowledge and maybe even uncover skills you did not even know you had. Once you have done this, revisit the goals you wrote down at the end of Chapter 4 and now transform these into what I call "stackable goals." When you examine your list of goals from Chapter 4, do some of these goals complement each other? In other words, can you identify or breakdown the goals you've selected into complementary goals that build upon one another?

Here is a simple example of stackable goals. My umbrella or overall goal is to swim from Havana to Key West. I am not a professional swimmer, but the corresponding stackable goals might be something like this: strengthen my rotator cuff muscle (by doing the assigned daily exercises), streamline my stroke, shave one second off my current time, etc. Each of these goals is a stackable or complementary goal to the previous one. When you accomplish one of these, it enables you to move in the direction of accomplishing the next one. Overall, this *Life Lesson Moment* exercise is inviting you to identify your key existing assets and then to go on to work more efficiently with each one by focusing on attaining complementary or stackable goals. This, dear reader, is an example of working smarter and not harder.

How to Work Smarter, Not Harder

One of the greatest myths in business is that you have to work hard in order to succeed, but the truth is that you have to work smart. Every business can become more successful by following some simple guidelines and rules of efficiency. Why reinvent the wheel when you can repurpose the fruit of your previously accomplished labor? Streamlining the way you work will free up more time for you to experience and taste the beauties of life.

Action Steps

Don't start from scratch. Stop reinventing the wheel. Reuse and modify resources already at your disposal. Leverage the work previously completed by other people to reach your goal. Are there ways you can modularize the key areas of your business and use them over and over again in slightly different ways? Can you identify the areas of your business where your existing resources, such as people capital or technology for example, could be maximized to accomplish even more with less?

Remain aware of how long each task takes. Your ability to schedule and prioritize your tasks depends on your knowledge of the time it takes to complete them. Take a moment to identify your most important recurring tasks and determine how long each one takes to complete. Are there tasks that could be completed more quickly? What would it take for you to cut back on the time it takes to complete them? Manage your schedule effectively and use your awareness of the time factor to schedule responsibilities effectively.

Prioritize tasks. List your daily goals, then identify your to-do list. What are the tasks you are going to accomplish today? Divide them into three categories, if possible: critical, high-priority, and low-priority. Tackle each task one by one in order of priority.

Stop, look, and listen. One of the greatest approaches I have put to work in my own business is my ability to stop, look, and listen and build upon the existing assets in my life. Are there skills you have learned as a direct result of field experience in your business that you can apply to new areas of your business? Are there resources you have acquired along the way during your recent tasks and projects that could be used more effectively to achieve your current goals? Lastly, as you examine the lessons learned at the end of each project or set of tasks, remember to not linger on mistakes. Simply continue to learn from your failures and move on.

Focus on your target market. Being good at servicing a set target audience is a very important aspect of every successful business. Who is your primary audience? These are the people who represent the bread and butter of your business. Who is your secondary audience? Identify the people who do not represent the majority of your clients but who purchase your services from time to time. And lastly can you identify the new emerging target audience you'd like to reach but have yet to successfully do so? These are the people who can become your clients but still need some efforts on your part in order to successfully serve them.

Innovate and look for new opportunities. Knowing your target market well does not mean you need to stagnate. The market is in constant flux. Are there new avenues in your industry or niche sector that you have not yet explored? Take a moment to identify new possible horizons for your business. The successful businesses are those that can anticipate changes in the market and dive towards new horizons. Maybe there are types of services you could be offering that target a new emerging audience. What are the opportunities in innovation on your horizon?

Work within your own cycle. Your best work will be performed when you work at your own rhythm and within your own cycle.

If you're a night owl, do most of your mundane work at night and keep your high productivity for daytime hours. Figure out the times when you do your best work and schedule your day accordingly.

Do what you do best; delegate the rest. Everyone has a perfect set of strengths and areas of expertise where they shine. Make the most of what you do well and ask for help or hire others when it comes to accomplishing your most challenging tasks where you have to use your weakest skills. Spend more time on what you do best. What are your strengths and what are your weaknesses? Are there ways you can fortify your character flaws? Or are there tasks that you would do best to simply delegate to others who excel at these? Draw up a map of your gifts and vulnerabilities and assign your set of tasks accordingly.

PART FIVE

Achieving Self-Actualization

According to Maslow, only 1 percent of people reach self-actualization. What is self-actualization really? What does it look like? Our definition could be our ability to reach our full potential, to be able to rise to the ultimate benchmark of our own making, and to be the best we can possibly be. The best parent, the best husband or wife, the best professional—not in the world, but in our world.

CHAPTER FOURTEEN

Self- Actualiza-tion—Do What You Love, Love What You Do

When you have responsibilities and you are not happy in your day-to-day life, it affects your family and your primary relationships. Just as your work contributes an economic value to your life and the lives of your loved ones, your happiness or unhappiness contributes an emotional value that affects their happiness or misery in return.

This Is Not My Life—This Is Drudgery

According to Maslow, only 1 percent of people reach self-actualization. What is self-actualization really? What does it look like? One definition could be the ability to reach one's full potential, to be able to rise to the ultimate benchmark of one's own making, and to be proud of the person we have become. Self-actualization represents that elusive lifelong process of turning into the best person we can possibly be. The best parent, the best husband or wife, the best professional—not in the world in general, but in *our world*.

In the last of Maslow's five phases of development and achievement, self-actualization represents that ultimate level we strive to reach before taking our last breath. But the levels of our lives are circular in nature. There is not just one area of striving for success, but multiple levels at once. When I had my clothing stores, I was striving to make money. I rarely came home for dinner with my family. I might have been making progress in the financial success category, but what about my ability to find love and a sense of belonging? What about my self-confidence? What about developing my personal and familial relationships?

Of course, being self-actualized, in part, means waking up every day and going off to work to a career that you love—a career that fulfills and engages you fully. There are many of you who wake up every morning and say, *This is not my life; this is drudgery.* Maybe you're a mortgage broker, or you own a clothing store like I did. Maybe you're in real estate or a lawyer or accountant. Regardless of your profession, somehow you've allowed your life to go off course. Many of my clients who have met with me and caught glimpses of my life have closed their eyes and thought, *Wow, maybe I should explore new horizons.* Up until that point, they were getting their paycheck on the 1st and 15th of each month—coming in like rain. Many of them had the courage to take a risk and make a change. Now don't get me wrong, I am not saying that the only way to have a fulfilled professional life is to be an insurance agent like myself. In fact, someone's misery might be someone else's delight and vice versa, but you must live the life that you *choose* and not the life that you *fell into*. Do what you love; love what you do.

When I drive down the freeway, I look at people going off to work and I always wonder how many of those people are truly fulfilled professionally and how many go to a "ball and chain" job. I've spoken with many who are less than happy at work and they will often say, "I am working towards retirement." Here's my response to those who live for weekends and for retirement, "What you really want to do is have the *option* to retire. But for that to happen you have to have the economic wherewithal to secure your future so that if you want to work until 68, great. And if you want to work until 78, that's fine too. Either way, you will have options to do what you want to do when you reach a certain age. But to work at an unfulfilling job and only start to enjoy your life once you get to retire is a travesty. Life is too short to start living on the weekends.

What Did You Dream When You Were a Kid?

Some people have no idea what it looks or feels like to work in a career they love, so making a change in that direction seems daunting and impossible. If you're among the many people who have no idea what you would love to do, think about the following anecdote from my life.

When I was that 11-year-old kid delivering papers, I had no idea what or who I wanted to become as an adult but I knew that I wanted to feel the way I did when I rode my bike through the neighborhood. That feeling I had was my inherent desire for self-reliance. But what does an 11-year-old know about self-reliance? I remember pretending I was the captain of a ship navigating dangerous waters. Trust me, sometimes riding my bike through traffic on Overland Avenue in Los Angeles did resemble navigating dangerous waters. I fantasized that I was a hero, like Sammy Baugh, the football champion of that era. Nobody was telling me what to do or what not to do. Riding a bike is a great freedom. You're out there. The grown-ups are in a car. Well, I have my bike and I'm jumping off curbs.

I may not have had a specific dream of what I wanted to become in those earlier days but what I did have was the feeling of freedom wired into me. What I loved more than anything in the work that I did is the absolute feeling of freedom I experienced throughout my career. Riding that bike through those streets of L.A., tossing papers on doorsteps, I was in charge of my destiny. I was the captain of my ship. And that feeling never left me.

Even as a kid, I was a person who really did what I needed to do in order to do what I wanted to do. And what I wanted to do was have adventures.

One day my friend and I hitchhiked to the San Fernando Valley. We just hit the back roads and we hitchhiked our way through the Valley. All I wanted was to see the world. Several hours into our journey, the police stopped us because we were just kids. And just like that, we had to go back.

Everywhere I turned in those early years, I yearned for freedom. Every winter, snow would cover the top of the San Bernardino Mountains, which I could see from my house. I would daydream looking at those snow-covered mountains.

"Dad, I want to see the snow!" I'd say to my father watching the mountains in the distance.

"Paul, we'll go next year."

I was 30 years old the first time I experienced snow.

If you're anything like me, and like most of the kids growing up today, you may not have had a specific dream of the person you wanted to become but you must have had a feeling of what made you feel *right*, what made you happy and content. Maybe you had that feeling when you were helping others at your local church on Sunday or while building something in your backyard. Whatever it was, every kid and every person recognizes the feeling of contentment, even if they don't know what form that contentment might take. As you consider developing the first or second career of your life and doing what you love, make sure that you follow your heart and create a life for yourself that will bring back that feeling of contentment you felt when you were a kid. If you are among the millions of people on this planet to dread Sunday nights, then close your eyes and go back to that time in your childhood when you felt free and playful. What were you doing when you felt this feeling? Now choose a career that allows you to experience that feeling and you will be on your way to doing what you love.

Bring Joy into the World

Not everyone is destined to become a brain surgeon or the president of the United States. Being fulfilled and being number one in your life can mean doing what some might consider to be the less glamorous jobs. Do you think that I thought selling insurance was a glamorous job when I first heard about the opportunity from my friend Hershey? The truth is I didn't. But guess what? This work ultimately became the life that brought me fulfillment and abundance beyond my wildest dreams.

I loved my work so much that Sunday nights I could barely sleep. Monday would come and it would be the day when I did the most business, out of any other day of the week. When I tell people about my inability to sleep on Sunday nights like a kid on the eve of his birthday, they would often look at me and say, "What's wrong with you?" The reason why most people didn't understand my excitement is that the majority of folks out there are depressed on Sunday nights because they hate their jobs and they feel trapped. Do you want to know why I loved my job so much? Because I knew that every life I touched, I improved tenfold. Do you know what an incredible feeling it is to know that your work is bringing peace of mind to your clients?

I have a client who sold Coca-Cola machines to offices. He loved doing that. He would travel to various offices of 30–50 employees and he'd make each one of those people happy by selling them cold Coca-Colas. He would say to the boss, "You know, it's only a nickel a Coke." This guy loved his job because it made people happy.

There are many reasons why people are not happy in their job. Perhaps they jumped into a career too quickly when they were young and did not allow themselves to experiment long enough. Perhaps they told themselves that the option they fell into was the only option they deserved. Whatever the case may be, it is important to remember youth should be a time of experimentation—a time to act on new opportunities.

Make the most of your youth, if you still have it, in order to discover what makes you happy. Take the time to unravel what makes you passionate so that when Sunday night comes around, you're filled with excitement because you can't wait for the week to start. If you're young and you've come across this book, you might be asking yourself, *Why am I not successful?* I suspect that one of the reasons is that you're not in the right occupation. You have not yet put yourself in a place to be successful.

Many Jobs, One Feeling

I realize today that in all of the jobs I had and liked in my life, from delivering papers to driving an ice cream truck, to owning my clothing stores or selling insurance, all of these jobs have one thing in common: They all required the need to develop relationships and provided me with self-reliance—being able to work at my own pace while feeling free.

Driving the ice cream truck, I was stopping all over the neighborhood and chatting with every person who bought an ice cream from me. I saw these people every day, because I had the same route. Even in those early days, I was a relationships guy. I felt connected to people. I was building relationships to increase my business. The more people I had on my route, the more income I would derive. When I delivered ice cream, they would say, "Oh, there's Paul." I had an identity. I loved talking to people even if it was only seconds while their kid played kick the can. I liked people then. I like people now. When I worked in the clothing business, I met interesting people. I built relationships with all of the customers who came into my stores. As you can see, the jobs I loved most are the ones that allowed me to connect to other people. This was not the case when I worked on the assembly line at Carnation where I was isolated and confined.

This wide range of work experiences made me realize that in order for me to feel fulfilled in a career, I would need to work in an environment that allowed me to interact with people. I am a relationships guy through and through.

Some people are born with a natural talent. You know, the lucky few, who as children already knew that they were here to invent the computer or write a symphony or win a sports tournament. These people are rare. Most of us go through life unsure of the path ahead.

People ask me if I imagined living the life I have now when I was a kid. Are you kidding me? Nothing could have prepared me for the lifestyle I experience on a daily basis now. The measure of my success today far exceeds the boundaries of my boyhood imagination. I didn't dream it because I had no models to reflect this life. I knew that everybody worked and that was what was expected of me. I didn't dream of money or of what I would become. Of course, I did appreciate the money, but more importantly, I loved the freedom the money gave me. As a kid, I had a Christmas account where I socked away one dollar a week, and then when Christmas came, I had saved $60. It was pretty nice. But never did I dream of leading the magnificent life I lead today.

As I write these words, there is a technician in the other room working on our electric shades. Do you think that when he was 21 years old, he thought, *I want to stand on a ladder and install shades*? Most people in life just "do." They just do. It goes back to the people on the assembly line. Many of them don't question their lives. But denying yourself a fulfilled life requires a lot of numbing. I would suspect that most people who lead a life of great discontent do whatever they need to do to become numb so they can get up day after day and go to a job they dislike.

As you consider moving in the direction of doing what you love, remember that the best time to make a change in your life is right now. So if you're ready to make that change and finally do what you love and love what you do, then I suggest you act on it today.

Decide to Make a Change: Unconscious Visualization

Most of the changes we make in our life begin with an unconscious visualization. Meaning that a moment comes when you say, *I want to control my life.* In that moment, you're not actually sitting there saying, *I visualize myself in King Arthur's Court*, but instead you know that you're not content with your life and that you want to make a change. This is the first step in the right direction towards making a positive change in your life.

Many of you reading this book might relate. You might be sitting at your desk with that salary-cap job of yours feeling the ball and chain around your ankle, right? And now you reflect back on that meeting you had with this person whose life you want to emulate. Maybe you look out the office window and see him drive away in your dream car. You might say, "Wow, he lives in that beautiful house? Oh my goodness, he travels to Hawaii each year?" That very moment when you finally acknowledge to yourself that you want to make a change in your life is the moment of unconscious visualization. This is the opportune time to make the change that you desire.

Go for the Goal: Conscious Visualization

Some of you might know exactly what you want to change. In fact, you have visualized yourself in great detail living in King Arthur's Court. This crisp visualization of the life you'd like to create is an example of conscious visualization. This is the moment you decide to go for your goal. This is a very powerful tool for making a change in your life. You might be thinking: *I don't like where I am. I want to be in King Arthur's Court. Can I do that?* I say, go for it!

Whether you're consciously or unconsciously visualizing what you want in your life, I know this about you: You want the same thing that Dick and Jane want; you want the same thing that everyone wants. You want health, and you don't want to get up on the first of the month and wonder, *How am I going to pay my bills?* If you are a married person and have children, you want to have enough money to have lox and bagels on Sunday, hire a babysitter, and go out to a movie. You don't want to worry about making a car payment. Maybe you might even want a new car. But being fulfilled is more than making more money. Yes, money is freedom. Let's be honest. I'll ask you this: Do you think that doing a job you loathe makes you free, even if you're well paid to do it?

Remember my story about the pineapple sherbet when I worked for Carnation? So I know what it's like to do a mechanical job that does not bring fulfillment. I've asked myself this question: Would I be fulfilled if I were getting paid $1 million to work on the assembly line at the Carnation factory? The answer is "no"! Do you want to know why? Yes, the money I would earn would give me some freedom, but I would not have the peace of mind of doing what I truly love. Without peace of mind to be myself, I would not be completely free nor would I be content.

Life: Assembly Required, Death Included

As you put your life together, assembling all of its various pieces, you will find there are two values of a life. The first one is the economic enjoyment—simply put, the amount of money you contribute to the world economically over the course of your life. In the insurance world, this is the death benefit or the monetary value we can measure. But the second measure of a life—which no amount of money can ever replace—is just how much you enjoyed your life, and how your presence in the lives of your loved ones contributed to their well-being and emotional happiness. As we assemble our lives, putting its various pieces together, we can say in all certainty that death is one component that has been included in this life kit of ours—the inevitable end that we cannot escape, no matter what we do. Knowing this fact, shouldn't we do everything in our power to enjoy the ride along the way?

When considering making a big life change in order to do the work you love and love the life you're living, many of you who have children and other dependents feel that these big responsibilities prevent you from making a change. You might say, *I can't take the risk because if I fail, what will happen to my kids?* To those among you who speak these words, I ask, "How can you afford not to take a risk?" For the sake of your children, build a life you love. Show your children there is a possibility that goes beyond the jail sentence of an unfulfilled job. Do not procrastinate. When are you going to take a risk? The 12th of never?

When you have responsibilities and you are not happy in your day-to-day life, it affects your family and your primary relationships. Just as your work contributes an economic value to your life and the lives of your loved ones, your happiness or unhappiness contributes an emotional value that affects their happiness or misery in return. Let me now ask you the question again: Can you afford to not make a change in order to build the life that you love? I think we all know the answer to that question at this point.

How Much Is Your Life Worth?

I can't tell you how many times I've asked my clients this simple question: *How much is your life worth?* The answer to this inquiry is a metaphor for how you plan on building your dream career. When I'd sit down with a client to do their financial planning, I'd ask them that very question. I'd say to them: If you were to die today, how much money would you want your family to have after you're gone?

How much is a life worth? The crude reality is that with a spouse gone, you need to know how much money the family would need over the next several decades to lead a quality life and educate the children. And to you, dear reader, I would like to ask you the same question: "What worth do you put on yourself? Are you going to live up to your full economic potential?"

Asking someone the worth of their life seems like a simple enough question, but clearly this has been one of the toughest things for people to answer. When people think about that question, they don't take into account all of the things that go into building a life. Here you are working day in and day out, taking care of your family, and, overnight, all of the security and the comfort that your presence brings them could be gone. I hope that as you plan for a new career, you consider the answer to that crucial question.

We can send a check to a family when a loved one dies, but we can't replace their role and the joy and the love that a mother and father bring. Technically, our mortality should be motivation enough to live an authentic life that aligns with who you really are and what you really love. But the reality is that most people live their life as if it were a dress rehearsal, thinking they have all the time in the world to live their actual life later on down the line. Again, don't procrastinate!

I can tell you today from the perspective of a 78-year-old man that life passes in an instant. You're 25; you blink and you're 40. You blink again and you're suddenly my age, contemplating the balance of your life. Would you like to look back and pave your old age with statements like "I wish I had…" and "If only I had done…"? The answer is "no." Nobody wants to look back on a life unlived.

When a client dies, sadness is there, of course, but I also feel such a sense of goodness knowing that I have secured that client's family for generations. There is no check that is ever too big. I understand that my work is saving families and it is this feeling that brings fulfillment to my professional life. How will your work improve the world and the lives of others?

Be Proud of the Person You've Become

If you were a guest at one of my homes, you would quickly see that I have achieved a modicum of financial success. I have all of the wonderful trappings that money can buy. The view alone that I have from my desk here in Los Angeles is worth more than a thousand words. So one day, I said to my wife, "You know, look what we've built over the years. Look at what we have achieved. Why is it that you have never come up to me and said, 'Wow, this is good!'?"

Do you know what my wife answered?

"It never occurred to me that you would do any less."

Her belief in me strengthened my self-esteem. Today when I look back on my journey, I realize that I have created a life for myself worth living—a well-balanced life of service to others and personal fun. Let's face it, I love opulence and comfort. I also know that in addition to creating a life of wealth I've also shared a great deal of my time and my treasure with others. Service and personal pleasure should not be mutually exclusive. I have both.

When I look back on all of the joys of my career, I see a long list of my clients who cumulatively have purchased over $2 billion of insurance over the course of my career. I love knowing that long after I am gone, somebody will get a check because of the work I did. The work I did for 40 years still affects lives today and will continue to do so tomorrow and for many generations. The measure of success is being able to enjoy the fruits of your labor all the while enhancing the lives of the people in your life and in your community.

Do what you love and love what you do. Live your life with intense happiness and experience passion in your work as well as in your personal life. How do you do that? Wake up every day and start doing what you need to do, so that you are able to do what you want to do.

As I look at my life, I feel an immense sense of pride in my legacy and in the person I have become. If my departed family members and friends could look down at my life, they would say, "You did good, Pauly." As I revisit the key points of my life today, I can say, *This is good, this is right, this is the way it should be.* There is no doubt in my mind I have reached self-actualization.

Life Lesson Moment

Dear reader, some of you might feel a bit discouraged by Maslow's statistic of 1 percent of people reaching self-actualization. If that is the case, I would like to remind you of Diana Nyad's incredible story of swimming from Havana to Key West at the age of 64. We can safely say that Diana did not have the odds in her favor when it came to reaching the goal of swimming 110 miles in shark-infested water. And yet what was Diana's mantra? *Find a way!*

Take a moment, dear reader, to visualize what your self-actualization looks like. Where are you? What are you doing? I spoke with a middle-aged author the other day about her vision for her self-actualization, and she said that she could see herself in her 60s giving talks in front of very large audiences. This is just one image in this person's visualization. What do you see in yours? Let us remind ourselves that this last phase of absolute success is layered and circular in nature, meaning that it engages every aspect of our lives, not just our work. As you bring your vision of your successful self to mind, are you surrounded by family and friends? Do you feel fully engaged with your community? What are some of the ways that you are a contributing member of society?

If you're met with thoughts of doubts and negative outcomes, repeat Diana Nyad's mantra, *Find a way!* But finding a way is not just a saying that is repeated endlessly without any daily actions to back it up. This is a good time for you to revisit your goals for this year and look at the tasks required for you to get there. When Diana reached the shores of Key West, she did so on her fifth try. And yet, each of the four times before when she fell short of her goal, Diana said that she was utterly shocked when she realized she had not yet succeeded. She was shocked because each time she endeavored to make that monumental swim, she was filled with an unshakable conviction that she would succeed. And each day before that great day of victory, she trained and worked and trained and worked and accomplished all of the million-and-one tasks that took her to her final goal.

As you visualize your full-fledged self-actualization, dear reader, carry that image with you every day. And most importantly, find a way!

How to Consciously Connect to Your Purpose

Connecting to your purpose on a regular basis is crucial in making sure that you are staying on course with realizing your dreams. Have you ever meandered aimlessly through a city, allowing yourself to go from shiny distraction to shiny distraction? It's fun and I suggest you give it a chance sometime, but don't conduct your entire life or career with that kind of meandering spirit. Stay focused on the prize and keep knocking off the goals from your list to ensure that you remain on target every day to manifest your vision.

Action Steps

First identify what you want. Before you can uncover your purpose, you need to clarify exactly what you want to bring into your life. Put it in writing so you can read it every day or anytime you need a reminder. Here are some examples that may resonate with you: I want to have more money than to just pay my bills. I want to feel excited to start the day when I first wake up. I want to feel freedom throughout the day. I want to be of service and to make the world a better place. I want to love my work so much that I feel like I am playing all day.

Time travel back to your childhood. If you're at a loss for how to recover your sense of purpose (or perhaps you are discovering it for the first time), take a trip back in time to when you were very young. What brought you the most joy before you bought into false beliefs? Did storytelling bring you to life? Or did you love to dream up inventions that could someday change the world? Or like me, did human connection make you feel alive and purposeful? Tuning into what first sparked your joy long ago often can inform your direction in life today.

Retrace your steps to the point you lost your way. Your life or career has somehow veered off track. Retrace your steps to where you began going off course away from your dreams. Was there a point where you stopped striving? Did you take a shortcut that you knew was wrong? Or did you simply never give your dreams a chance and picked a career path you never liked in the first place? Gain wisdom from your past mistakes and avoid making the same bad decisions moving forward.

Remember that the past is over and done. Now that you have retraced your steps and have a clearer idea of where you might have made a wrong turn, let go of any guilt, fear, or superstition you may feel about your life prior to this point. The past is gone, and it has zero to do with your future or what you are capable of today. Remind yourself of this fact over and over as you proceed. Write down the things you'd like to let go of and tear up or burn the list as you let each item go in your mind.

Practice conscious visualization. Most of the time we don't consciously visualize the lives we want. Actually imagining your ideal life path is a powerful tool in making it a reality. Many people make the mistake of focusing on what they do not want instead of skipping right to the good part and visualizing what they *do* want. Be specific in your daydream. Don't censor yourself with fearful thoughts or perceived limitations. Allow your dream to be as massive and as magical as it once was when you were a kid.

Tap into what is most important to you today. What are you passionate about? Is it social justice? Helping others feel financially secure? Changing the world through innovation? Is there any way you can merge your values and beliefs into your existing journey? Take some time to identify all of the key ways where you feel passion and would like to focus your efforts.

Leave your comfort zone. Your comfort zone is not going to help you achieve anything but comfort. You have to constantly soul search and take on new roles in order to grow. Your purpose will most likely be discovered through a series of trials and errors. So get rid of the idea of being comfortable, take a few risks, and challenge yourself to discover the unchartered territory where you would like to take your business.

Remember there is always a way. Maybe you haven't figured it out yet, but rest assured that there is a way to bring your purpose and your current life into alignment. Remind yourself that you haven't experienced everything yet, and that the doorway to a purposeful life of meaning and fulfillment could be just around the corner. Take a moment to consciously explore unexplored opportunities. Are there people you should be contacting or risks you could be taking? Don't let yourself become paralyzed. Go into action mode now.

Take the time for self-care. Respect your body, mind, and spirit. Relax with activities like: listening to music, taking a walk, soaking in the bath. Taking good care of yourself is a sign of sound physical and mental health. After all, your health is the foundation of your success. Even if you're facing health challenges, work with the hand you've been dealt and do everything you can to work to your maximum abilities.

Embrace an attitude of gratitude. Be grateful for what you have right now, instead of what you don't. Developing a daily gratitude practice has been proven to improve quality of life. It also helps you to focus on the positive elements in your life and to capitalize on the things you can change and build moving forward. Make a list of at least three items for which you are grateful upon waking or right before bed.

Be authentic. You need to be honest with yourself about who you are and where you want to be. Acknowledge your shortcomings and flaws first, before you can work on overcoming them. It was Oscar Wilde who said, "Be yourself; everyone else is already taken." Are there areas of your life where you are not being as authentic as you could be? What are some changes you can make today to move in the direction of deeper authenticity?

Ask the right questions. Self-awareness is required to achieve your vision. But many of us don't ask ourselves the right questions to uncover what we truly desire. Example: *What skills or qualities do I need to work on to be more proud of who I am?* Take a moment to ask yourself tough questions about who you are and where your life is today in relation to your all-time dream. Are there elements you need to address and change right away? If so, do it now!

Review your purpose daily. Take the time to review your purpose and see if you're still on track with the realization of your dreams. Write down a set of daily affirmations you can post around the house or your office to remind yourself of your dream. Things like, "I am golfing each morning before I get to the office on a course overlooking the ocean in Hawaii." Be specific, don't be afraid to dream big, and remind yourself on a daily basis of the dream. Don't forget to check in with yourself on a regular basis to see if you're still on course to bring your full vision to fruition. There is no time to waste.

CHAPTER FIFTEEN

On Giving Back and Leaving a Legacy

Someone recently asked me what I believe happens after we die. I believe that I live on in the deeds that I have accomplished during my lifetime, and that the energy that I have contributed to the world through my work survives in the legacy that I have built.

Leave a Legacy Behind

One day, I meet one of my dear clients for lunch in West Hollywood at Michel Richard's, which is a great restaurant. He was a partner at a renowned entertainment law firm here in town. I get to the restaurant, which is off of Melrose, a very lovely restaurant with valet parking. In those days, I used to carry a man's purse, which was ridiculous. First of all, for me to have one was a terrible idea because I always lose everything, but also the idea of a man's purse in itself is pretty silly. Anyway, the valet is getting ready to take my car. I put my hand on my seat to get my little man purse, and… gone! Oh no! I left it in Santa Monica. I look to see if I have any money in my pocket and I have NOTHING.

I go into the restaurant. I sit down. About two minutes later, my client arrives. I say to him, "I left my little man purse in Santa Monica. I don't have the money to pay the parking attendant."

"Don't worry, I'll take care of it."

"Great, what about lunch?"

He paid for everything. I loved this client.

Shortly after our meeting, he died of a heart attack. He was 48 and married with two kids.

Life isn't fair. The one thing that brought me any comfort in this client's situation was knowing that the service I had provided him ensured the security and well-being of his family. The reality is that it is not *if* something bad will happen to one of our loved ones or us but *when*. Over the years, I built a career I love, founded on lifelong relationships with my clients whose well-being has remained at the center of my focus. I know that in the four decades of business I conducted as a successful insurance agent, I provided the best product in the country. I knew that I was doing something great for every single one of my clients. Thanks to my career and the services I provided my clients and their families, I helped them weather the financial storm ahead. In many ways, my career has enabled me to leave a magnificent legacy.

On Giving Back

In the last phases of self-actualization comes the desire and the ability to contribute to charity. Perhaps this is the ultimate measure of success, this *metamotivation* as Maslow calls it, that turns us beyond the self in order to contribute our time and our money to further the well-being of our communities at large.

When I was a little boy, there was a blue and white charity can in the house—it was called the *tzedakah* box, which in Hebrew literally means "justice" or "righteousness." In spite of how things were for us financially—and they were never rosy—there was always something in our *tzedakah* box. Giving was part of our culture growing up.

It was something that we did, regardless of income. I grew up believing that there is always someone out there who has less than you, so giving is a necessity. Giving is what I've done my entire life.

One of the ways that we gave when I was growing up, in addition to our tzedakah box, was to a series of charities like the March of Dimes. So once a year, I'd come to school with ten dimes to donate. Charity was always in my mindset.

The concept of "tzedakah" goes beyond the bounds of traditional charity. In Judaism, giving is an obligation that is typically understood as a gesture of goodwill. Even those with small incomes contribute, as my family and I did when I was a kid going off to school with my ten dimes. Contributing to charity is a way of life. It doesn't matter whether you're making $20,000 a year or $20 million a year—you can contribute to charity either by donating money or by working as a volunteer and giving your most valuable asset: time.

Teach a Man to Fish

The well-known medieval Sephardic Jewish philosopher Maimonides said that the second highest form of tzedakah is the anonymous gift, while the highest form is the gift, loan, or partnership that will result in the recipient supporting himself instead of living off others. There is nothing like the feeling of giving to charity and knowing that your money is helping your community and the future of the world. Many universities are highly supported by philanthropic contributions. As you walk on a university campus, you can see the names of donors on buildings. Think about the idea of donating scholarships for underprivileged and gifted students, ensuring that gift will go on in perpetuity. Those kids who will attend college on your contribution and become productive members of society will have the advantage of giving back to the world at large. There is nothing more gratifying than the act of giving.

Because Joyce and I highly value education, we have funded a series of scholarships for students attending Brandeis University.

Education is the ultimate empowering gift that affects the entire life of its recipient. The creation of these scholarship funds is our way of affecting multiple generations to come. We have been so fortunate to receive so many wonderful letters of acknowledgment over the years from students expressing their gratitude for the support we provided for them by way of these scholarships. I will never forget the day when Joyce and I were attending a fundraising event. There we were, wearing our nametags, when a woman walked up to us.

"I am the parent of one of the recipients of the Joyce and Paul Krasnow Scholarship Fund," the woman said to us. "And I want to thank you from the bottom of our hearts for your generous contribution. After Brandeis, our daughter graduated from rabbinical school and became a rabbi. If it had not been for your help, she would have never been able to attend college."

The joy, the pride, and the fulfillment Joyce and I felt and still feel today knowing that our contributions enable young people to further their education is unlike any joy we have ever experienced.

Although I am a generous contributor to countless charities, I have to admit that I have not given anonymously. I enjoy the recognition. I know I shouldn't. I feel a little strange about it. But I am being honest: I like it. I suppose there is an inherent human trait to liking to be recognized. But I have not been able to give anonymously. Call it vanity or call it pride, but I would like my name to be up there still after I die.

Charity has expanded my world and brought me to live through enriching experiences I may not have had otherwise. Joyce and I support a multitude of charities all over the world. Being involved in these charities has added another dimension in our lives. We have met some of the most interesting people whom we would have never come into contact with otherwise, from great musicians to great architects. It has been a fascinating road that has enhanced our own lives beyond measure.

The best part of it is that we give to charities where we can see the impact of our donation, in other words we can concretely visualize how our gift has added a little brightness to someone's life. I like to know where the money goes. Some organizations have such heavy administrative costs, rendering the gift abstract. I try to select organizations whose administrative expenses are low so that the largest percentage of donations goes to the actual recipients and not to run the organization.

When you think about it, how much wealth does one need? Recently, 31-year-old Mark Zuckerberg and his wife, Priscilla Chan, gave away 99 percent of their Facebook stock to charitable causes by creating an organization called the Chan Zuckerberg Initiative. When asked why and how they can bring themselves to donate an estimated $45 billion, the power couple said they wanted to improve the lives of the next generation including that of their recently born daughter, Max. Their primary areas of interest are education, curing diseases, and building strong communities.

While being interviewed about the monumental decision, Zuckerberg recently said in an interview, "The only way that we reach our full human potential is if we are able to unlock the gifts of every person around the world."

Like Zuckerberg, Joyce and I believe that we have a moral responsibility to donate to causes and programs that help improve our world so that future generations can come to learn and experience more than we ever could.

Although there have been other wealthy people like Bill Gates and Rockefeller who have donated a large portion of their wealth, donating 99 percent of one's wealth is actually unprecedented. I deeply admire Mark Zuckerberg and his wife, Priscilla, for their unparalleled generosity. Obviously, Joyce and I did not donate $45 billion like the Zuckerbergs, but we continue to stretch ourselves in relation to our income in order to give.

The Joy of Giving

Someone recently asked me what was one of the greatest challenges of entering retirement, and I answered without hesitating that I miss being able to donate as much as I used to do at the peak of my career. Joyce and I live the most wonderful life; we travel to the most beautiful places. But the pleasure of giving to students, whose lives are changed, far outweighs the pleasure of a wealthy lifestyle. It's not what you have in life that makes you a whole person but how you live and how you see the world. When it's all said and done, how much wealth do we really need in life? Once we've satisfied our basic needs, we can now literally change the world by giving to charity.

Andrew Carnegie is a perfect example of the power of charity. Most people probably don't know that as one of the richest persons in the world, he ended up giving more than 90 percent of his wealth away to charity. Carnegie believed in the Christian concept of the "Gospel of Wealth" that stated that wealthy people were morally obligated to give back to their community. His wealth allowed for the creation of more than 2,000 libraries as well as the creation of a $125 million foundation called the Carnegie Foundation to aid colleges and other schools. Carnegie represents one of the highest examples of selfless giving. I have not even come close to giving as much as Carnegie, of course, but for some reason, I want to leave a legacy and an imprint on the world that will outlive me. In short, I want to be remembered for something that is deliciously good, and that enriches and improves society. Donating to charity continues to bring me experiences that have continuously broadened my life.

What Is Your Legacy?

As you establish your goals for your business, make sure you set yourself up for leaving a legacy of good deeds behind you. It took me a long time to realize just how important my work was to my clients, and that I was a life and family changer. I wish I'd realized that sooner. I wish I'd known the beneficial impact I was having on the lives of my clients and their families.

Today, as I write this, I am 78. I probably won't be here when I am 97. But whether I am or not, I can say, *Look at the thousands of lives that I have affected. Look at the billions of dollars that will continue to pour into these people's families. I know that after I am long gone, there will be great-grandchildren attending Harvard because of my work.*

I've often asked myself what happens to us after we die. I believe that we live on in the deeds that we accomplished during our lifetime, and that the energy that we contributed to the world through our work survives in the legacy we built. And if we have children, our legacy shines on for one-and-a-half generations. Our actions and our love for our children will carry on for the duration of their lives and that of their own children—one-and-a-half generations. I believe that my legacy is going to be the good deeds and the good works that I have done on this earth. That legacy is my heaven. I believe that our goodness should take place while we are on earth. And I believe that we should follow the Golden Rule that states, *Do unto others as you would have them do unto you.*

So, long after Joyce and I are gone, students at Brandeis University will sit down in the science computer library and see a plaque on the wall that reads, *In gratitude to Joyce and Paul Krasnow.* They might not know who those people are but maybe, just maybe, they will think of our names in gratitude. Either way, I will have enjoyed giving during my time here on this earth and I know that what I've done for the community over the years—whether it is giving to the Jewish Home for the Aged, the Weizmann Institute, the Skirball Culture Center, our synagogues, Brandeis University, or being on the board of the Northwestern Mutual Association of Agents—by giving back has been a gratifying experience. I have had a great career and I've given back to the company and to my fellow agents at Northwestern Mutual in countless ways, including being the president of the Association of Agents all the while being in the top 20 of our company and working full time. The impact of the charities to which we donate will outlive us.

Life Lesson Moment

Dear reader, take a moment to think about how you would like to be remembered and what you would like your legacy to be. Students in creative writing courses are sometimes asked to write their own obituary. Most of these young students cannot begin to acknowledge let alone understand the concept of their own mortality, and yet this exercise invites them to look beyond the narrow view of only what is in front of them.

Regardless of your age, I am inviting you to write your own obituary. You might feel that this is a morbid exercise, but I am here to tell you that clearly and consciously envisioning and crafting the legacy you would like to leave behind is nothing short of life-affirming and empowering.

As you begin to put pen to paper for this exercise, focus on what you would like your legacy to be. How were you a contributing member of society during the course of your lifetime? How did you positively impact the lives of loved ones and strangers alike? What were your contributions in your field, but also in the world at large? Were your core values clearly communicated to those experiencing your loss, through the power of your actions during the course of your lifetime?

Once you're done with the obituary, read it carefully. How closely does your current life reflect the key events and values communicated in this obituary? Are there things that you need to begin working on in order for this legacy to not only come to life but also exist beyond your own existence? Lastly, take out your list of goals for this year and for the years to come and see if you need to revise them in order to bring this legacy to fruition.

As you read your own self-crafted obituary, you are fully empowered, dear reader. Your life is truly your own.

How to Give Back

Giving back to your community and the world at large is an essential part of being a whole and successful person. I cannot stress enough how enriched I feel by all of the charity work I have done through the years. Find charities to support, donate your time, and donate your money. The worlds and connections that will open up to you as a result of being of service to your community will far outweigh the value of your donations.

Action Steps

Support other businesses in your area. Cross-network with other companies in your community. This can help you reach more people and help out other local business owners at the same time. The cross-pollination of working with other businesses in your area can be a powerful way to create new avenues for your business and others. Identify the businesses in your area and contact them to find ways to connect, collaborate, help each other out, and simply become a part of each other's networks.

Lend an ear. Learn to be a good listener. Something as simple as being there for someone and listening to their problems. The better you listen, the more solid your connections and relationships will become, which in turn will result in a more enriched life with countless new opportunities awaiting you. Are there ways you have not been a great listener lately? Can you remedy this situation right away and become a better listener today?

Sponsor a youth sports team/club. Connect with a local youth sports team or club and find a way to sponsor or support them. You can also extend your sponsorship to other local organizations. What are some of the local organizations or teams you can reach out to today and sponsor?

Show your appreciation. Write a note to an employee or colleague. It is so easy to criticize but how often do we omit sharing praise with the people around us? Are there people in your office or in your life in general for whom a letter of appreciation is overdue? Expressing gratitude for someone else's work and efforts always enriches the relationship.

Offer your skills. You likely have an area of expertise that's of value to others. Consider teaching classes to local residents or offer to teach a specialized skill to those who are out of the workforce. Are there organizations in alignment with your mission and industry where you could offer your services such as sitting on a board or giving a talk?

Support others' interests. Find out what causes your employees care about most. Allow them to vote and select a charity to which your business can donate.

Encourage employee volunteerism. Many businesses are now offering paid time off for volunteering. Give employees a specific amount of time each month, quarter, or year for volunteer work. Or designate a day for companywide volunteering. This can boost morale while also increasing a business's community involvement.

Organize a food or book drive. Launch or sponsor a book or food drive in your community. You can also organize a fundraiser for the organization of your choice and invite the people in your networks to attend.

Share others' success. Celebrate others' achievements. Let them know you noticed their good work. Hold an "employee-of-the-month" nomination or simply give your employees a gift card and a personalized note to show that you recognize their contribution or success in your business.

Mentor a student. Connect with a local school or Big Brother, Big Sister organization in your area and mentor a student. The impact your efforts and energy can have on a young person can have positive effects on them, visible for generations to come.

CHAPTER SIXTEEN

What Is the Measure of Success?

When *Roger Bannister became the first athlete to run a sub-four-minute mile, we measured his success and declared him number one. Roger happened to beat the world record at that time, but most importantly, he beat his own record. Roger ended up running faster than Roger. The goal in our quest for success should always be focused on surpassing ourselves, more than surpassing others.*

Finding Food and Shelter

As we approach the end of our journey together in this book, I'd like to revisit the monumental question: What is the measure of success? We now have the vista of the years of experience I've shared with you to place this question in a different context. How would you now define the measure of success in your life?

There are several ways of measuring success. Economic success is the most obvious measure that sometimes misleads people into thinking that if you make a lot of money, you must be successful. Would you tend to agree with that? I would not. Yes, of course, the trappings of my financial success are very enjoyable and they certainly show, on some level, a modicum of success, but they don't even come close to representing the fullness of my accomplishments. Success is more than money; it also includes the ability to build safety and security, to connect with others, to develop self-confidence, and most of all, to reach self-actualization.

When I was a young man owning my four clothing stores and building my business, if you'd asked me back in those days whether or not I thought I was successful, I would have told you "yes." I thought I was a big shot, but, in fact, I wasn't. My ego was the size of the Grand Canyon, and yet we all know by now what happened in 1974 when I went bankrupt. But let us play out a scenario and imagine for a moment that I never went bankrupt. Let's say I had been able to sustain that amount of business through the years and was able to hold on to my stores. Would I have been considered successful? The answer is simple. No. Why? Because my life in those days could not have been more out of balance. I never had dinner with my family. The stores would close at 9:00 p.m., and by the time I came home at 10:00 at night my kids were already asleep. By the time I woke up, my kids had already gone off to school. I met my eldest son, Marc, at 13, when he became a bar mitzvah. Not literally, of course, but I was not physically there for his childhood. I was working constantly. In those early years, I was working so many hours that the truth of the matter is that I never had time to spend with my family. This is a sadness that will stay with me forever. If I could not be a present and loving father to my children, how can I say that I was successful in those early years? I was not. So if economic achievement is not the ultimate measure of success, then what is and how do we go about getting it?

Nepotism or Inheritance: Two Ways to Become Rich

Years ago, when I was 18, I read a wonderful article in the *Christian Science Monitor* outlining two methods of acquiring wealth: nepotism and inheritance. Well, if that were the case, then I was out of luck because I certainly didn't have major connections in my early years, and I most definitely was not going to inherit any money. Luckily, I did not read that article and say, *Well, there is no chance for me.* I read it and thought, *Well, that's their point of view. There must be other ways to build wealth.* I agreed with the main idea of the article stating that it would be difficult for someone to start from nothing and pull themselves up by their bootstraps. But *difficult* never scared me. When I went on to build my insurance business, I did it through the power of referrals and networking. Being referred to a prospective client does not mean that you're pulling the nepotism card. Of course it's not. Nepotism is having your father be Louis B. Mayer, who then hires you to be the CEO of his great Hollywood empire, MGM. Many successful people in America prove the thesis of this article wrong. I know so many people who are self-made. And by self-made, I don't mean that no one helped or supported them along the way, but rather that they built their business on smart and consistent work over many years.

I met a number of wonderful people who sit on a prestigious university's board of trustees. Many of these folks are self-made, while some of them came from wealth. Do I think it is wrong to inherit? Of course not. I would have loved to have inherited money. When I started out in my business and needed $15,000, I had to convince investors to risk their money. Inheritance would seem like a much smoother and less risky path for sure. Would I have liked it better for my father to have had this huge insurance practice for me to take over? Absolutely! I would have loved that. Hard work is great but there is nothing wrong with inheritance. Most people don't have that, however.

Everything in our society has a measurement. In education, testing and contests are among some of the assessment methods. So we can proudly declare statements like: *My third-grade class is in the top quartile* or *Wow, I won!* In business, these equivalent assessments determine whether or not you are a success in your industry. But are those measurements important?

Remember our discussion of Elizabeth Brinton, the number one Girl Scout cookie salesgirl? Here she was, putting herself in the most populated spots, like metro stations, so she would sell the most cookies, in the shortest amount of time. She sold more than 100,000 boxes of cookies! So, yes, measurements are important, because if we don't utilize these metrics, then how do we know what we have achieved? The criterion of achievement is of course more complex than counting the number of boxes of cookies or calculating the number of sales in any given business. We've all gotten on the scale in the morning and have seen that number thinking, *Oh no, this is not the measurement I want. I'd like 20 percent less, please.* In the end, we can measure certain elements that give us an idea of the overall evolution of our progress, but is that the only measure of success?

When I could hardly sleep on Sunday nights, I couldn't wait to start my workday on Monday and continue striving for my own sense of success. Here is what I thought: *I want to be number one in my mind. I want to be number one in my environment.* When you're a salesperson, your success or failure is measured every day, but the reference point of where you're starting off compared to where you want to end up is the only thing that should matter in that scenario.

When Roger Bannister became the first athlete to run the first sub-four-minute mile, we measured his success and declared him number one. Roger happened to beat the world record at that time, but most importantly, he beat his own record. Roger ended up running faster than Roger. The goal in our quest for success should always be focused on surpassing ourselves, more than surpassing others. The absolute measurements of success are self-referential. In other words, it is about setting up your own benchmarks and figuring out how much you are progressing in relation to *yourself* and not others. This takes us back to our push-up principle. How many push-ups can you do? How many would you like to do? The measure of success is ultimately an internal process, rather than an external one. Success comes to people in different ways. In the end, it all comes down to perspective.

Measuring Personal Progress

When I am in Colorado looking at the Rocky Mountains, I can do so from the base or from the summit. My experience and what I am able to see around me will shift, depending on my shifting perspective. Whether we're looking at the mountain from the summit or the base, there is no "right" or "wrong" perspective but rather the angle from which you choose to look at the world. Each reality is in fact equally beautiful but ultimately quite different, each affording me a wealth of information unlike its counterpart. There are beauty and perspectives all around us. If you're measuring your own progress, all that matters are the starting and ending points. Success is measured in your own heart and in your own soul. That's why you get out of bed in the morning: to outdo yourself and to progress. The rest is irrelevant.

Establishing Safety

It is clear by now that financial success is not everything. In fact, establishing a clear, solid foundation of safety in your business is one of the measures of success. Certainly, bankruptcy is a perfect example of the negative consequences of failing to establish a sense of safety in our own business environment. But what do we mean by safety in this context? I am not referring to the elusive safety net—which as you know, I do not believe exists. Instead, I am referring to "minding the store." In my case, this was meant quite literally. But in more general terms, ask yourself, *How safe is my business?* How far are you looking ahead and are you putting yourself in a position to ensure that this financial success continues beyond the early years of your operation?

The Safety of Your Environment

I've attributed a lot of my success to being able to see a different perspective. Being nimble and thinking fast on my feet and changing in mid-action to make a new decision based on the shifting circumstance saved me many times. This was certainly the case when I was giving that presentation in the conference room facing Mount Rainier. The key is to be able to set your ego aside and allow yourself to say, "Gee, I didn't realize that." This ability to embrace that kind of level of humility and willingness to change the course of your day or your career will allow you to make the appropriate decisions for your shifting environment. This nimbleness can yield a better life, not just professionally but personally as well.

When people disagree and they argue with each other, they might say, "How can you believe this?" But if you take a moment to step back and realize that everyone has a different perspective, then it is easier to understand how someone might not think the way that you do. Perhaps now is the time to knock down those old walls and create new pathways. The key to being able to gain a different perspective is to align yourself with people in your life, mentors and experts in their fields, and expand your world to create new horizons. In my own career, I've always had a mentor or two. There are many ways and places where you can go and get help. There is always someone with a different perspective or who might know more than you do. Even if you don't agree with people in the end, you might learn by viewing things from their point of view. As long as people are not harming themselves or others and are contributing to society, it is irrelevant whether I agree with them or not. I want to do business with people who have a global rather than a narrow view of the world.

Location, Location, Location

We've all heard the old adage in business of "location, location, location." There is nothing truer. Once you've set sail into the adventure of building your own business or career, you have hopefully established a very clear sense of the clientele you would like to target. Remember when I realized I had to shift my primary clients from doctors to business managers? That was an important change for my career. The question I'd like to ask you is this: Have you put yourself in a position to become economically successful and build safety? If you're selling diamond rings at Zales at the mall in your hometown, that's one thing, but if you're selling diamonds at Cartier in Beverly Hills, that's another. Who has a better opportunity? You have to put yourself in a place where you can have the opportunity to move forward economically and build more safety for your business. Change your environment. Remember that it might take me more effort to sell you a Ford Fusion than it takes me to sell you a Bentley. Do you know why? Because the people who can afford a Bentley will not hesitate to make a purchase. Who has the dollars to pay my fee? Once I have answered that question, those are the people I need to target.

There is nothing more important than having a clear sense of who your dream clients are and then going after them. Our young Girl Scouts entrepreneur Elizabeth Brinton knew that already at age 13 when she declared that identifying and understanding her clientele was one of the reasons for her success. Well, okay, yes, she was not exactly a typical 13-year-old girl. Not every child sells 100,000 boxes of Girl Scout cookies in their free time. But we can all learn something from this basic principle of knowing your clients and putting yourself in the environment where you will be able to connect with them and establish a clear sense of safety in the environment of your business.

Finding Love and a Sense of Belonging

The third criterion of success falls in your ability to find love and establish a sense of belonging in your life. This is an interesting conundrum for many businesspeople and most specifically for businesspeople who are also parents. We often feel pressured to work harder and therefore spend less time with our families in order to succeed.

But is an alienated worker with dissolved personal relationships after a divorce or broken friendships an efficient worker?

Prior to 1974 and the entire implosion of my business, our clothing stores were open seven days a week. My priorities were skewed; I did not have the maturity to prioritize. I worked constantly. I lived like that for too many years. If there were a Maslow meter of success measurement that would calculate my involvement with my family in order to calculate my overall success in my business life and my life overall, I would certainly have been deemed a failure. Those early years were not easy. I was not "Dad of the Year," believe me. It's especially not easy realizing that I did all of that and still went bankrupt in the end. All those long hours went for naught. I wish I had read my own book back then, so that I could have had a chance to be a better human. The outcome of my life would have changed significantly. But that's not how life works. We do the best we can. The truth is I can't say that I did the best that I could because I did not know what the best was. Nor did I know what I should do. It's not easy to be a father. There is no University of Dadhood.

Here's the difficult thing about the trajectory of our lives: We can't get back the time we wasted in the past. The most difficult thing to accept is knowing that I wasted so much of my children's formative years. No matter what I do, or how successful I am today, I can't get that time back. I wasted 12 years of my life. Nothing I can do or say today can give me back those years. And in the end, I ended up going out of business anyway. These are difficult truths to accept.

And then bankruptcy happened and it felt like someone had shot me in the head with a cannon ball. I guess that's how it feels when crisis hits our lives. Overnight, I made the radical change of starting to have dinner with my family every night. Even if there were times when I had to go back out and meet with clients or attend business-related events, I would come home and have dinner with my wife and kids. What's more important than that? Nothing.

When my daughter was in middle school, much to her chagrin, I was the chaperone on many of her school trips. This was something that was very important to me. I was there for all of those events for her. When my son Eric was in the marching band in high school, and they'd go to their competitions in the sports arena downtown, we were at every competition. I made that shift consciously, because I have learned from my past mistakes and I did not want history to repeat itself. I looked at my life and said, *This is not good.* I made a radical shift after I began working at Northwestern Mutual. The time that came before that was a crisis. It was a clear-cut moment in time.

Dear reader, how many years are *you* going to waste?

Building Your Self-Confidence

The third criterion of success is our ability to build self-confidence in our business and personal lives. When people don't succeed, it's not that they say, *I don't know how to do this* when the opportunity comes knocking, but rather it usually is a problem of self-confidence where they say, *I am afraid to do this.*

It is very important to accept that you can accomplish your goals. Telling yourself that you are able to do something and that you can in fact succeed is not "faking it" as some people might think. The ability to develop a strong sense of self-confidence comes with the ability to accept that you can in fact do what it is that you are setting out to do.

My background brought me to make internal changes as a result of external factors in my childhood. Rather than saying to myself, *Wow, look at how difficult things were when I was a kid*, I accepted those factors and moved forward.

Obviously, some people are able to establish a strong sense of self-confidence while others are not. The bottom line is this: Are you telling yourself that you're being the success that you want to be? Are you telling yourself that you're worthwhile? Are you telling yourself that you're talented and contributing to another person's life?

Reaching Self-Actualization

Many people get lost in the first four areas of achievement of their lives before even being able to consider getting started on becoming self-actualized. Struggles with money or relationships leave many of us caught up in all-engrossing battles that drain us of all of our energy. Remember the story of the waitress who received that order of a sandwich with lobster instead of bacon and gave up and went home? Fear can be a great motivator for some, and a paralyzing factor for others. If you are in the minority of people who become self-actualized, you will be challenged to work and grow and expand your horizon in each of the main areas of your life. This includes the areas of providing food and shelter, developing security for you and your loved ones, building and maintaining engaging relationships, and developing a solid sense of confidence. All of these have to be addressed before you can begin to tackle self-actualization.

A large part of self-actualization means adding value to the lives of others and leaving a legacy behind. One of my favorite stories about my participation in charity was the day when I went to the Jewish Home for the Aged in Los Angeles and met with the CEO. We were visiting the brand-new Alzheimer wing, which houses people suffering from this terrible disease. As you can imagine, this wing is highly secured. You have to be buzzed in when you enter the premises and you have to be buzzed out in order to leave. This precaution is to protect, of course, the patients and prevent them from simply slipping out and wandering off into the streets of Los Angeles.

So, here I am in the lobby, waiting to meet the CEO, when I decide to use the restroom. I open the door to the men's room and walk in. Inside the men's room, I see an elderly lady. When she sees me, her face lights up with excitement and she says, "Ooh, I knew if I waited long enough, a man would walk in!"

Where do you have wonderful experiences like that?

The way to success is paved with so much more than good intentions. The way to success is paved with hard work in every single area of your life. A truly successful person is a whole person.

Life Lesson Moment

Dear reader, the time has come for you to take a look at Maslow's pyramid of hierarchical needs once again. Now take a piece of paper and draw five columns at the top of your page. For each column, write down one of the five areas of Maslow's needs, beginning with physiological and ending with self-actualization.

Find a red pen and a blue pen. In blue, write down the accomplishments you have managed to bring to fruition in each of the areas of your life ranging from physiological need all the way to self-actualization. In the red, write down the things you would still like to accomplish in each of those five areas but have not yet addressed. Write down as many things as you can. Take your time in completing this exercise. Your page would look something like this:

Physiological	I work out regularly. I am healthy.
Safety	I own our beautiful home. My business has saved enough capital to weather an economic storm.
Love/Belonging	My marriage ended.
Esteem	I am a respected member of our church. I am a good parent.
Self-Actualization	The various areas of my life are fulfilled.

When you're done, what do you see? Is there more blue or more red ink on the page? What are some of the top priority areas in the red category that you need to start working on this year, this month, this week, today? Now, return to your obituary and your list of revised goals and check to see if you have to further revise the list of goals one more time.

As you go through these various exercises, you will be crafting a multi-layered strategy and a plan of action for your own success. As long as you continue to work on these goals and remain engaged with an action plan, you cannot lose your way. At the end of each calendar (or fiscal) year, revisit the various exercises in this book and update their content. As the months and years progress, you will see your list of accomplishments moving from red to blue, each time a bit closer to reaching full self-actualization. This, dear reader, is freedom in the making.

How to Measure Your Own Success

Success is a subjective lens—one person's definition of success may not be your own. Make sure you take the time to clearly define your own vision and the finish lines you would like to reach along your journey. Don't be afraid to set your own standards, away from the fold; identify what is important to you; and raise your own bar to the level that feels right. Ultimately, the measure of your success is your very own.

Action Steps

Set your own standards. Quit judging yourself according to other people's definitions of success. Define how high you want to raise the bar and make your choices accordingly. Beware of the distorted reality portrayed on social media. Stay focused on your own values and life and stay the course. Remember your lifelong commitment to yourself and your success. Take a moment to jot down a description of *your* standards for success.

Identify what is most important to you. Get specific. Have a clear picture of what you want in life and how to go about achieving it. What are you not willing to give up? What do you want to bring to life and what are the elements in your life that are no longer serving you and you are willing to let go?

Raise the bar. Are you selling diamonds at Zales but would like to sell diamonds at Cartier in Beverly Hills? Raise the bar for yourself. Don't be afraid to set your sights higher and avoid settling for the low-hanging fruit. What are some ways that you can raise the bar for yourself? Are there goals you have been afraid to set because you worried they were not achievable? Can you imagine reaching for the stars instead of just reaching for the neon lights at the gas station?

Make a difference. Give back to your community, family, and world at large. What legacy do you want to leave? Take a moment to think about your legacy and write your own obituary. This is an excellent exercise in thinking about the ways you would like people to remember you and therefore trace back your steps to the path you'd like to follow to that ultimate finish line.

Understand your passion and your skills. Recognize what you are actually good at and merge it with what you want to do. Take a moment to create a grid of your passions and match each one with a skill or a set of skills. What do you see? Are there passions that do not have skills and vice versa? Can you solidify your grid by creating even more connections and matches between these two categories of skills and passions? The more you connect what you love with what you're good at, the more you will create opportunities towards a fulfilled life.

Build quality relationships. The quality of a relationship can be more important than the number of relationships you have. Are you someone people can rely on? Are you a good listener? Are you a good friend? Who are the people with whom you have the most solid, quality relationships? Are there steps you could take today to solidify some of your relationships and bring them to a higher standard of quality?

CHAPTER SEVENTEEN

Being a Whole Person

Einstein said, *"My religion consists of a humble admiration of the illimitable superior spirit who reveals himself in the slight details we are able to perceive with our frail and feeble mind." When they send rocket ships to the moon and beyond, do they encounter heaven? Or do they just find more outer space and more planets? Where is heaven? I do not know if God exists. I don't question it. What I believe in is being a good person. I believe in ethics and morality.*

I sat down with one of my wealthy clients when he was 60 years of age. We were doing a review of his policies. I said to him, as I have said to many of my clients, "Here is a palette of paint. How would you like to envision your life when you're 65? What do you see?" His answer surprised me: "I want to acquire more buildings."

I thought about his response long after we had finished our conversation because it led me back to my musing on the measure of success. If we're lucky and gifted and smartly working enough to be among Maslow's 1 percent who have reached self-actualization, then our achievement spans far beyond financial success and into other areas of our lives—ranging from providing food and shelter all the way through being motivated by more than just finding security, or even connecting and loving others or establishing the strong roots of our self-confidence. One of the measures of true success must be, in fact, the ability to be a whole person. But what does that mean? What does being a whole person look like?

When I asked my client to use paint to create the entire palette of his life for the next five years, he could not come up with anything but the desire to build more wealth. It made me realize that he, like many people, had gotten addicted to just acquiring more. Caught in the treadmill of the empty space of acquiring without realizing that they are missing the joy of life. Being a whole person is a sharing, giving, building, living, learning experience. The joy of life certainly is not just acquiring more. Is it? Maybe it is for some people, but then what did it all mean by the time you reach the end of your life—aside from an arsenal of buildings and money invested all over the world? The truth is that there is always someone out there who has more than you do. Always.

Over the years, I have prided myself on acquiring my art collection. Remember the Chagall I purchased? Well, there have been many more acquisitions since that one, and while I deeply enjoy looking at our art, I recently met a man with a monumental art collection that simply dwarfed our own. He and his wife hosted us at a dinner party in his home in Boston. There is always someone out there who has more than you have.

At the end of your life's journey, what matters are the variety and the number of facets of the adventures you have taken along the way. We are composites of our years on this earth. It is the complexity of these experiences that makes you the whole person that you are.

There are so many components that render an individual a whole person. Ultimately all of these assets can be rolled into one giant snowball and we can only hope that it will get bigger and bigger as it picks up more momentum going downhill. Isn't life better if lived with variety? Personally, I want to hang out with people of all socio-economic strata. Why not? Most people have something to offer and something to add to my life. Why would I hold back and miss out on what they can teach me? Do I want to miss going down the Pacuare River on a raft in Costa Rica? Do I want to miss riding my bike through the fall colors? Do I want to just sit and watch others? I want to taste everything and have these exponential life experiences that flood me, rather than a narrow view of the world and what is possible.

I have a lifetime of stories to cherish. I'll never forget our hilarious trip down the Pacuare River in Costa Rica. Joyce and I traveled with two other couples. Here we were sitting on this rickety wooden bench waiting for the oldest plane in the world to pick us up—a DC-3, left over from the World War II days. The airport was nothing more than a shack with a grassy field as the runway. When we boarded the ancient plane, there was no air conditioning. It was hotter than hot and so humid; it was like being inside the mouth of an elephant. As the plane was getting ready to take off, I looked outside of the tiny plane window at the bench where we'd been sitting and saw our luggage sitting there! No one had bothered to load it onto the plane. Seconds later we were in the air praying for our lives and hoping we'd arrive in one piece, while trying to forget that we would be arriving without our luggage. These are the adventures of a lifetime.

I also remember our trip to Borneo, where I held an orangutan. Oh my, do you know what that feels like? When I reach the end of my life, I don't want to conclude that I've forgone living extraordinary experiences for the sake of making even more money. The reality is that there is only so much money you can spend.

So let's go back to the passages of life in your early years. This is the time to become a person of interest. First, there is a clear benefit to being a layered and nuanced person with outside interests: The fact is that people want to be around you because you're interesting. When you allow yourself to become a multi-faceted individual, perhaps you will be able to say: I gave a building to my alma mater, or I just provided 25 scholarships to deserving students. Or yet again, I gave my church that fantastic organ or I supplied 100,000 Bibles to people in Africa. This is what makes you a whole person.

What are your interests? Are you fulfilling them or are you waiting for tomorrow? Maybe you're getting ready to run a marathon, or coach your kid's Little League team. Maybe you're bringing a symphony orchestra to a part of the world where there is none. Are you meeting your buddies for lunch in that hole-in-the-wall restaurant that has the best sandwich you've ever tasted? The key is to bring value to your life so that you can share that value with other people and the world at large.

One of the reasons why I feel so comfortable sharing this advice of striving to be a whole person with you is perhaps because I was not such a whole person in my younger years. I worked relentlessly throughout my youth, often to the detriment of my family. Who out there can reach beyond the years of their life and say without a doubt that they have not made mistakes?

Through the years, as I progressed in my own evolution, I have had to forgive myself for my own transgressions. I believe in apologies and I believe in forgiveness. If I do something wrong and I want forgiveness, I believe in saying, "I transgressed against you. Please forgive me, even though what I did was odious. Please accept my apology." There are of course some things in the world that are unforgivable. Things that nobody can forgive, like crimes against humanity, such as the mass genocide in Rwanda, the Holocaust, or the Boston Marathon bombing. Personally, I believe in the powers of apology and forgiveness.

Even beyond the ashes of unforgivable crimes, there is hope and there is life. Years ago, I traveled to Auschwitz with a group of people from our synagogue and visited the concentration camp. Many people visit Auschwitz. It's not a fun place to visit, as you can imagine. Here we were, 90 people sitting across from the crematorium ovens where they sent people to their death, when all of a sudden, we hear a beautiful melody in the distance. We listen closely and realize it is *Hatikvah*, the Israeli national anthem. *What is going on?* we say to ourselves. We all turn to see who could be singing and around the corner come 150 Jewish kids carrying a large Israeli flag stretching across the span of the children—their melodious voices rising above the ashes where millions of Jews lost their lives under the most heinous conditions. Tears were flowing among us, as we listened to the melody of *Hatikvah,* a song that means "hope." I'll never forget that moment in life.

Ultimately, it is the manner in which we conduct our lives following the mistakes of our actions that is important. How do I care for my dog? Am I kind to my neighbor? Am I a good provider? Do I live my life as a whole person? Do I respect my family? These are the only things that matter at the end of the day. I hope you will learn from my mistakes and you will embark upon the path of becoming a whole person.

Memory and the Power of the Past

I find the past to be enormously helpful. I believe that life is a series of linked memories. There is beauty in remembering great experiences. When you arrive at the end of your journey, what will your memories be? If you're lucky enough to live a long life, you will strive for its passages to be fulfilling and meaningful.

It is up to you to take care of yourself mentally and physically. Your body is sacred, and you need to treat it as such. Your mind needs constant stimulation. It is important to take time to develop interests outside of work. Look at yourself and ask the questions: *Do I have a balanced life? Do I want each day to be an adventure filled with the excitement of a fulfilling career? Do I experience all of the joys that life has to offer?* Hopefully the answer to these questions is a resounding yes. A whole person is not made only of work; it has been scientifically proven that people who do not have hobbies and activities start to decline much more quickly than a person whose life is totally engaged. This is the reason why it is extremely important to develop friendships, outside interests, hobbies, and activities that actively engage your mind throughout your entire lifetime.

When I look back on my life, I have a whole series of memories that bring me joy *and* I have interests today that keep me as engaged and excited as I was on those Sunday nights when I couldn't sleep from the anticipation of the exciting work week ahead. I may have semi-retired, but my level of engagement and excitement have not waned one bit.

My memories of holding an orangutan in the Borneo rainforest or walking with gorillas in Rwanda are experiences that not only bring back fond memories, but have really engaged me in activities regarding the saving of our planet and endangered species. The past is a great map of where you're going in the future. Why wouldn't I want to remember the good, the bad, and the ugly? Memory is a powerful tool for growth.

While I find the past to be an incredible teacher about myself and who I have become today, moving forward is great; but I don't want to forget where I came from, because then I'll never know where I am going!

Invest in the Capital of Your Health

Joyce's father died at 95. I don't think a green vegetable ever passed those lips. When he cooked his meat, he used to show it to the flame. There are many people who smoke and don't eat a single green thing and they live to be 100. A friend and great gentleman named Burt we had dinner with the other day was 102 years old and started out dinner with a big shot of bourbon. And there are some people who exercise their whole lives and are health fanatics and end up getting the worse ailments in the world. A lot of that is genetics, but also a matter of the choices you make in your life. I am a strong believer in moderation.

There was a friend of ours who went to St. George, Utah, to a health spa. And after a week of balanced diets and sessions with health experts, the nutritionist takes everyone outside and says, "I am going to tell you something and if you follow it, you'll never gain a pound, for the rest of your life. But if you don't follow it, I cannot guarantee anything." Of course by this time, everyone is on pins and needles. They are about to find out the secret to remaining fit and thin for the rest of their lives. What is it going to be? Finally, the nutritionist looks at them and says, "If it tastes good, spit it out." Everyone laughed.

The key to health and a well-balanced life is moderation. Isn't life supposed to taste good? Why say, "I'll never eat another ice cream sundae again"? Just don't have one every night after dinner. Moderation is also about allowing time for every aspect in your life—your spiritual life, your educational life, your children, walking your dog, your exercise. You have to have time for everything. But it's difficult when you're 35 years old, and you have a family, and you're building your career.

When I was 40 years old, I started exercising. Until that point, I had never exercised. I resembled the cartoon character the Shmoo, with the biggest part of my body being my behind and stomach. I was a perfect hourglass shape. It wasn't a pretty sight. And then one day, like so many middle-aged people who first catch a glimpse of their mortality in their fourth decade, it dawned on me that if I wanted to stay on this earth longer than a minute, I'd have to start exercising and change my lifestyle. Today, I exercise every day. Whether it is by taking a long walk in nature when we are in Colorado or by visiting the gym when we are in L.A., I stay active. Staying connected to the needs and the well-being of your body is as important as making appointments with your clients. The main thing is to invest in the capital of your health, because without it, you have nothing. Taking care of your body is a major part of being a whole person.

The Golden Years

Here I am in my seventh decade. It happened so fast. I am telling you this because it seems like yesterday I was just in my 40s; I blinked and today I am 78 years old. Don't put off what you want to do until tomorrow because tomorrow is already here. I am living a new chapter of my life. When I look at my schedule today, I laugh because retired people are supposed to be able to lounge around and do much less. Joyce and I don't have a free day or a free night this week. We are so busy and so engaged in the activities of not just everyday life, but in the activities of the world. The Fourth of July parade is coming to Vail—it is a sweet and quaint hometown parade where our synagogue always has a float decorated by the teenagers of our community. The theme of the parade is "Decades of America." These are the types of events that we are engaged in on a day-to-day basis.

Last year, we hosted a fundraiser for the Bravo! Vail music festival with about 120 guests. One of the world's greatest maestros, Bramwell Tovey, played the most magnificent music in our home. The experience of witnessing the work of one of the greatest living conductors today in my very own home was an unforgettable experience. How do I stay engaged? How do I not stay engaged? It is during great moments like these that I can step back and look at the breadth of my life. I will never forget that night. The music was just wafting over us. It was so beautiful. And I remember thinking, *If only my mother could see me now.* My heart ached because I could not share these beautiful moments of triumph with my sweet mother whom I had always adored. Ultimately, we humans want to be recognized, not only for who or what we are but more importantly, for what we do and what we contribute to bettering the world. I would have loved to have my mother witness that magical evening, maybe because it was the culmination of my own success. Here I was sitting with my beautiful wife in our lovely home, with the breadth and depth of my rich career behind me. I was a loved man with the complex layers of my life intersecting in this moment. When my mother died, I was 29 years old, so many light years from the accomplishments of that evening. Not just because seven years after her death, I would lose everything, but because I had not yet come to terms with what was important in my life.

So, yes, I am constantly engaged, and this level of engagement with my life brings me a great deal of fulfillment. There are constantly people asking me, "Paul, can you do this? Can you help me here?

Can you be on the board of the interfaith chapel? Can you help us in our fundraising? Can you play golf? Can you take a hike?" I want to convey to you, dear reader, the richness and fullness of your own life. People and organizations call me for assistance in fundraising and participating in their lives on a daily basis. The fuller your life, the more you are in demand. But I have to take a step back from all of this activity and take time to myself to think, meditate, and spend time to regroup. Yesterday, I simply took care of myself by taking a day off from our very busy schedule. Our dog, Hercules, Joyce, and I took the best walk and when we came home, I took my little lounge chair, put it on the lawn and groomed Hercules. Then I deliciously read a book, went upstairs, and had a light dinner and watched the Tony Awards. This was a wonderful day of rest and leisure that even to this day, in the midst of my semi-retirement, I hardly get to indulge in. But the truth is that resting and taking care of yourself is not indulging; it is a fundamental part of a balanced life.

I have learned that it is important to give the mind an opportunity to have a day of rest. It is a fundamental part of having a balanced life.

I like to remind my clients to make sure they take the time to have date night. I like to tell them, "The kids need to know that mommy and daddy love each other and want to go out and spend time with each other. Your life is not only your children. They are part of your life." I really do believe that our children do not belong to us. Our job is to facilitate and guide their independence so they can go out into the world on their own. In the words of Kahlil Gibran, author of the wonderful book *The Prophet*:

> Your children are not your children.
> They are the sons and daughters of Life's longing for itself.
> They come through you but not from you,
> And though they are with you yet they belong not to you.

The quality of the life you lead by the time you reach your 70s is directly linked to the life you conducted in your 20s. When you're young, you may not realize that you are actually determining your golden years by the decisions you make around the following questions. Are you taking care of your physical body? Are you taking care of your spiritual body? Are you taking care of your mental body? Are you making sound financial decisions that will help you secure your future and that of your family? All of these elements come together to create that whole person; then you will be a person of completeness.

Spirituality

I am a very spiritual person. My spirituality has played a significant role in my development and my success and the person I have become. My notion of God is more anchored in the manner in which I am conducting my life today than in an actual definition of God per se. At every juncture of my life, I ask myself, *Am I doing the right thing?* This is a question that you must ask yourself daily.

When you are conducting business, you can do a lot of things that benefit only you and not your clients. That was never the way for me. I need to ensure at every step that I am conducting myself ethically. I know that if I choose the ethical path, I've got a client for life and I know that even if no one is watching. Maybe someone is watching; I don't know. But I am my own conscience. I do know when I do something wrong. I am aware of the moments when I am short with others or trespass against my fellow human being. We all have the ability to develop a moral compass.

No Regrets

When I look back on my life, the only regret I have is not having spent more quality time with my family in those early years. Making money is great, but you have to balance your life. In the end, you make money, you lose it to somebody else, and then you make more money again. Why wasn't I home more often? It is difficult, but I have no choice but to forgive myself for that and move forward. Today, I am a good grandpa and a good father. That's important to me. There doesn't need to be a conflict between making money and being a good family person. There is no shame in having money and living life to its fullest. Once again, the key here is balance and moderation.

There is joy in having luxury in life. When I travel to a city, I often call the concierge at one of the best hotels, like the Copley Plaza Hotel in Boston, and have them suggest some great places to experience fine dining. The last place they mentioned was a place called Limoncello on the North Side—a fantastic Italian restaurant, reasonably priced with a great house wine. The waiter came from a town just outside of Naples. And when I spoke with him, I learned that he was making about $50,000 a year while spending $20,000 to send his son to college. Before I left Boston, I made sure I gave the concierge a little envelope to thank him for his help, because everyone deserves to be paid. Everybody deserves to make a profit. Many people think they are the only ones who deserve to make a profit, sometimes at the expense of others. But I like to remember that a great deal is one where everybody gets something in the end, even if it means giving up a small piece of what you originally wanted. In a great deal, someone will always say, "I wish I had paid $100 less," while the other person will say, "I wish I had gotten $100 more." That's a great deal. I know people who have to win at all cost and who think, *I am going to grind this guy*. Although the pleasure of making and spending money is great for me, it never outweighs the other areas of my life.

I do not lose sight of my quest to always strive to be the best person I can be. This is part of the journey of becoming a whole and successful person. We are not talking about reaching economic success here, but I think that your success of living your life as an ethical and moral person increases your chances for economic success. It's going back to the definition of success and its many layers. At the bottom of the pyramid is the need for money, but the success of a person is measured by so much more than that. The key is to remain cognizant of one's actions on a day-to-day basis. How do I keep my conscience alive and engaged? I regularly assess my own behavior towards my fellow citizens. Every day in Colorado, I get up at 6:00 in the morning to let our dog, Hercules, out, and I watch the sun rise through the large bay windows overlooking the Gore Range surrounding our home. I am always taken aback by the profound beauty of the tangerine morning sky. This beauty never gets old; every morning, I gasp in surprise. Beauty is the gateway to my spirit; it is the one sure thing that allows me to connect to something greater than myself. This is my connection to the spiritual lens of my life. When I go to Florence and walk on the Piazza del Duomo and see the magnificent Renaissance dome of the Santa Maria del Fiore Cathedral, it takes my breath away. All I can say is *wow*! Or when I'm in India and I visit the Jewish sites, the old synagogues, my spirit stirs. Or when I go to Auschwitz and I hear those children singing among the ruins of atrocious pain. Beauty escorts me into the spiritual realm every single time. But I don't need to explain or define God or spirituality. It is too dense for me. It feels like trying to eat Jell-O with chopsticks.

Einstein said, "My religion consists of a humble admiration of the illimitable superior spirit who reveals himself in the slight details we are able to perceive with our frail and feeble mind." When they send rocket ships to the moon and beyond, do they encounter heaven? Or do they just find more outer space and more planets? Where is heaven? I do not know. I don't question it. I believe in being a good person. I believe in ethics and morality. I use the word "God" often. I like to say, "May God bless you." What I'm really saying is, "May you be a blessing unto yourself." Because isn't it our duty to bless ourselves? To be the captains of our lives? Are we not responsible for the course of our actions and for the deeds that we have done here on this earth? It would be nice to have unwavering belief, but the truth is I don't know and I don't question it. The world is too perfect for it not to have been some kind of divine intervention.

At the end of my journey, my life is my legacy. That is my heaven. And I believe that goodness should be created and shared while we are here on earth. Ultimately, I believe in following the Golden Rule.

Life Is an Adventure: Take the Journey!

As I write these words, I am watching a lady in a wheelchair at the edge of a lake. She must be in her 80s. Her adult children are standing beside her; one of them is securing her oxygen tank on the side of the chair. They have pushed her along this rocky trail so she could see the beautiful lake. She is frail and they pushed her right to the water's edge. From where I am sitting, I can see that she has a smile on her face. She is in that last passage of her life. And you know what she is doing? She is fishing! A man who appears to be her son is handing her a fishing pole and she is beaming because she is going on an adventure. Her son adjusts a pillow in her back; they are making her comfortable. A few droplets of rain begin to fall and the woman and her adult children remain unshakable in their desire for this moment. A young woman behind the chair reaches into her bag and pulls out a poncho and places it over the elderly woman who continues to smile as she proudly holds her fishing rod in the water. Do you know what this woman decided to do when she woke up this morning? She decided to stop, look, and listen. She must have said to herself, *Life is bustling around me. I see it, I feel it, and I want to be a part of it.* Life is not over until it's over. Life ends the moment you decide to stop exploring the million-and-one facets of your being; it stops when you're finished painting your life in its full range of palette colors, and not a moment sooner.

Life Lesson Moment

As you might have realized by now, I am an introspective person. I like to look at the various aspects of my life and make sense of what I've done and what I am considering doing. Some might say that I overanalyze everything. Whatever the case may be, I have developed a practice that I highly recommend to anyone who would like to stay on track not only with his or her day, but also with the course of an entire life.

The practice is simple. When I am out by myself walking the dog in the forest, or wherever I happen to be, I take a moment to reflect on my day by talking to myself out loud. Why do I like to do that? Because it allows me to ensure that I stay focused and in alignment with my core values. It is during this time of self-reflection that I ask myself tough questions: *Am I doing the right thing? Am I accomplishing what I want to accomplish today?* Sometimes the answers to those questions are not easy to face and I come to realize that I was not as aligned with my core values as I could have been or that I was not as clear or as respectful with someone as I could have been. Let's be practical; you are lucky to go through a day without making a mistake. What you can do is to realize what you did right and what you did wrong, so that you can be on the road to self-improvement. It is in my having these conversations with myself that I remain focused and on track, not just with my day but also with the overall trajectory of my journey.

As you move through your busy life, take a moment for self-reflection. You may not want to talk to yourself out loud, but feel free to adapt this exercise in the way that makes sense for you. This might come in the form of journaling or simply taking a walk and quietly reflecting or meditating. Whatever method works for you, take the time to ask yourself how your day is going. Are you on the track that leads you to the destination of your choice? Expand that question to determining what you would like your legacy to be. What would you like to leave behind at the end of it all? What actions can you take today, this week, this month, or this year to impact your life and the lives of others in a positive manner? Don't let your life get away from you, dear reader. Make sure you build in these quiet moments along the way to ensure that you are on the desired path of your choice, actively working every day towards your dream, all the while staying in alignment with your goals and core values. In the words of the American Unitarian minister Orville Dewey:

> "Labor is man's greatest function. He is nothing, he can do nothing, he can achieve nothing, he can fulfill nothing, without working."

Now put this book down and go out to create that rich fulfilled life and legacy worth passing on.

Now begin...

How to Become a Whole Person

Happiness and success are made of more than having a fulfilled work life and making a lot of money. The key to your success, and ultimately your happiness, lies in your ability to become a whole person. This means having a rich life in all areas of your existence. Is your family life balanced? Are you tending to your physical, mental, and spiritual health? Are you currently involved in your community? Do you think about the impact you will have had on the world once you're gone?

Action Steps

Keep your career in perspective. Your career can bring you tremendous purpose, fulfillment, and joy, but don't disrupt your life's balance by living exclusively at the office. Find work that you love, or learn to love what you do, but also be willing to expand your life so you can enjoy all it has to offer. Take a moment to jot down your key accomplishments and involvements in each of the following areas of your life: career, finance, health, family, friends, romance, spirituality, giving back. Are there areas where you are out of balance or need some tender loving care? Bring all of the areas of life back into balance by making sure you are not neglecting any of them.

Remain dedicated to your family and the friends you love. We all crave the connection of having a strong network of family and friends. Devote time to nurturing this support system, no matter how busy you become with your career. Keep a standing date for family time with kids, or prioritize date night with your spouse or significant other. And maintain lasting friendships by spending time with your nearest and dearest and showing up for them when they need you. These are the people who have been there for you during hard times and times of plenty, so it's important to always maintain strong ties with them.

Work to become a "people" person—even if you're not one naturally. Developing great relationship skills will serve you in all areas of your life because we live in a people-driven world. To improve your relationship skills, work on becoming a better listener in order to really hear what others are saying. If you're nervous when dealing with others at work or in life, focus on being interested—not interesting! This helps you feel more comfortable, because your attention is 100 percent on the other person instead of on you. Additionally, get feedback from your peers to get a sense of your performance; this helps you assess how others perceive you and can give you a sense of what skills you may need to work on. And finally, put in face time and maintain contact with clients, family, and friends alike. Over time, it will become easier to connect with everyone in your life!

Explore your spirituality. Spirituality involves your relationship with your soul and its place in the universe. If you wish, spend some time contemplating what spirituality means to you. There are many helpful books that can guide you on this journey. Other modes of exploration may include joining a house of worship, prayer, or meditation. Remember that you don't necessarily have to follow any specific organized religion or practice to reap the benefits of getting in touch with your spiritual side.

Find a meaningful way to give back. You don't have to write a giant check to contribute to the world around you. There are plenty of valuable ways to help others. Sponsor a runner in a race that benefits a cause close to your heart. Periodically buy food for your local food bank. Walk shelter dogs while getting your daily exercise. There are countless ways to improve the world; just look around and find something to do that's kind and benefits others.

Make time for fun. You've put a lot of effort into making your life great, so find a fun way to enjoy the fruits of your labors. Embrace a great hobby that helps you recharge after a tough day, like playing a musical instrument or painting. Take weekend trips to a nearby destination that renews you. Or organize a cookout and invite your friends over for an evening of food and fellowship.

Learn to really be present. One unintended side effect of excessive busyness is often the inability to be still and present and to be a good listener. But if you can master quieting your mind so you can truly be in the present moment, your daily life will improve. When you are present you'll find that it's not only easier to relax, but you'll also be able to achieve a deeper level of focus during intense work periods. Adopt a mindfulness practice that works for you, whether it's deep breathing, meditating, yoga, or taking slow restorative walks.

Notes

Chapter 3

1. Ludden, Jennifer and Weeks, Linton (May 26, 2009). *"Sotomayor: 'Always Looking Over My Shoulder'"*. NPR. Retrieved August 30, 2009.

Chapter 11

1. http://www.greenbiz.com/article/apple-google-tesla-and-race-electric-self-driving-cars

About the Author

Paul G. Krasnow is a financial representative at Northwestern Mutual Life Insurance Company, where he has been a top producer for 40 years. He is known for providing innovative solutions for his clients' personal and business needs. Paul has been named a Top 20 Agent 18 times and a Top 10 Western Regional Agent 25 times. Early in his career, Paul suffered a financially devastating bankruptcy with a line of clothing stores he owned, but went on to join Northwestern Mutual, where he has created an impressive financial portfolio and a strong network of clients, many of whom have become lifelong friends. Paul enjoys teaching others about the mindset of resilience and the skill set it takes to prosper in any environment. He has published articles for insurance publications both locally and nationally and has served on a variety of boards. Paul regularly speaks for multiple life associations in the U.S. and has given seminars for law firms and CPA firms in the Southern California area. For more information, please visit www.paulgkrasnow.com.

Let Paul Krasnow Teach You to Build Trust and Create Clients for Life

Survey after survey shows that trust is at an all-time low. People are suspicious of organizations, institutions, and leaders in every arena. What's more, competition has never been tougher. Clients can leave (at any time and for any reason) and replace your products or services with something faster, shinier, and sexier.

But here's the good news, says Paul Krasnow: When you're able to engage clients in the right way and build deeply connected, authentic relationships with them, you *will* set yourself apart. Clients will trust you. And once you have their trust, you'll win their loyalty, earn their referrals, and enjoy repeat business for a lifetime.

In his keynote presentation, Krasnow reveals the trust-building secrets that have allowed him to prosper. A few things audiences will learn:

- How to identify your core values and adhere to them in every aspect of your life and career (Hint: Krasnow's are integrity, client security, and hard work)
- Why you must never sell your clients products they don't need
- How challenging your clients with tough questions strengthens and deepens your relationship (and how to do it without alienating them)
- Why successful people think "clients first," not "income first"
- How to engage with clients and keep them engaged over a lifetime

- Why clients respond to authenticity (and what it looks like in action)
- How to make meaningful connections with clients in the age of technology
- Why keeping your word delights and impresses clients
- Tips for prioritizing loyal, long-term clients (rather than inadvertently neglecting them in favor of new ones)
- What it means to own your choices and actions and hold yourself accountable for them
- How to master a mindset of resilience that allows you to overcome losses, setbacks, and failures
- Why high expectations matter—and how to continually and relentlessly "raise the bar"
- Why you *must* take bold action even in the face of debilitating fear
- How to give and receive caring feedback
- How basic habits can be a game changer for long-term success

Krasnow insists it doesn't matter what industry you work in: Solid, trusting client relationships are *always* the cornerstone of a thriving business and a successful career. Let him walk you through the process of attracting the right clients and serving them in a way that keeps them coming back again and again.

To book Paul Krasnow for a speaking engagement, please visit www.PaulGKrasnow.com.